"Beautifully written with honesty and purpose, *Owning Bipolar* is a must-read for anyone struggling to understand bipolar disorder. As a practicing psychiatrist for the past twenty years, I have too often seen patients and families overwhelmed, scared, and confused when they first hear the diagnosis. Michael Pipich has developed an essential resource that will provide clarity and understanding to a seemingly complex and confusing psychiatric condition. Patients, families, and caregivers will be guided by the central theme of not being controlled by bipolar disorder but, instead, maintaining control and thriving. This book replaces isolation and apprehension with courage and hope. Ultimately, the reader learns that emotional stability can be achieved, and happiness, creativity, and control are not only possible but within reach."

—DAVID B. WEISS, MD, FAPA

"A comprehensive, inspiring, and cutting-edge guide. Pipich empowers readers so that they can eventually 'own' bipolar—which I believe is the missing link to effective lifelong mood stability. *Owning Bipolar* is a remarkably helpful, unique book. It makes me feel good to know it's out in the world, because I know it will help countless people affected by bipolar disorder."

—DYANE HARWOOD,
author of *Birth of a New Brain:
Healing from Postpartum Bipolar Disorder*

"*Owning Bipolar* is a practical guide for bipolar patients and their families, who often feel lost in myriad mental-health-system processes and services. It will expand your mind with evidence-based treatment modalities and allow you to explore the truth of your experiences. By learning the truth from Michael and from people who are on a similar journey, you can take charge of your bipolar, choosing state-of-art treatments and moving forward toward the emotionally balanced, productive life you deserve."

—GALINA MINDLIN, MD, PhD,
author of *Your Playlist Can Change Your Life*

"*Owning Bipolar* offers an essential biopsychosocial framework for understanding, taking control of, and living with bipolar disorder. This book should be read by everyone involved—not only people who live with bipolar mood swings and their families and loved ones, but also doctors and therapists, who can also learn a great deal from Michael Pipich's wisdom, born of immense clinical experience. I really would have appreciated having had a book like this when I was in clinical practice, both to read myself and to share with my patients."

—LINDA GASK, MD, emerita professor of Primary
Care Psychiatry, University of Manchester, UK,
author of *The Other Side of Silence:
A Psychiatrist's Memoir of Depression*

"Treatment providers and supportive family and friends can use the incredibly well researched and well-written information in this book to help shorten the gap between first onset of symptoms and effective intervention. My brother's bipolar condition proved to be fatal. I believe a book like this in his hands and in the hands of those who wanted to support him may have made the difference between suicide and an ability to sustain a passion for living. This book is essential reading, not only for the person learning to own bipolar condition but for the support-system members and treatment providers walking alongside in the journey to hope and healing."

—SALLY SPENCER-THOMAS, PsyD,
co-chair, Consumer/Survivor Committee,
National Suicide Prevention Lifeline, and
president, United Suicide Survivors International

owning BIPOLAR

How Patients and Families Can
TAKE CONTROL of BIPOLAR DISORDER

MICHAEL G. PIPICH, MS, LMFT

Foreword by Joseph Schrand, MD

CITADEL PRESS
Kensington Publishing Corp.
www.kensingtonbooks.com

To Jane, Adam, and Kevin

CITADEL PRESS BOOKS are published by

Kensington Publishing Corp.
119 West 40th Street
New York, NY 10018

Copyright © 2018 Michael G. Pipich

All Kensington titles, imprints, and distributed lines are available at special quantity discounts for bulk purchases for sales promotions, premiums, fund-raising, educational, or institutional use. Special book excerpts or customized printings can also be created to fit specific needs. For details, write or phone the office of the Kensington sales manager: Kensington Publishing Corp., 119 West 40th Street, New York, NY 10018, attn: Sales Department; phone 1-800-221-2647.

CITADEL PRESS and the Citadel logo are Reg. U.S. Pat. & TM Off.

ISBN-13: 978-0-8065-3879-2
ISBN-10: 0-8065-3879-1

First trade paperback printing: October 2018

10 9 8 7 6 5 4 3 2 1

Printed in the United States of America

Library of Congress CIP data is available.

First electronic edition: October 2018

ISBN-13: 978-0-8065-3880-8
ISBN-10: 0-8065-3880-5

Contents

· · · · · · ·

Foreword   vii

Preface   xi

INTRODUCTION: Nobody Is at Fault   1

1: Origins of Bipolar Disorder   9

2: Diagnosing Bipolar Mania, Hypomania, and Depression   19

3: Why Bipolar Can Be Difficult to Accept   39

4: Understanding the Bipolar Experience   53

5: Bipolar Therapy: A Three-Phase Approach   67

6: The Medication Conversation   85

7: Bipolar Medications   95

8: Thriving in Life After Stabilization   125

9: Postpartum Onset in Bipolar Disorder   145

10: Hospital/Inpatient Treatment   157

11: Need for Support from Families and Beyond   167

CONCLUSION: Going to the Next Level   199

Reference Guide to Bipolar Medications   203

Acknowledgments   219

Index   221

Foreword

· · · · · · ·

WHEN I WAS A GUEST on Michael Pipich's *Breakthrough* radio show in May 2013, Michael started the show by reminding listeners that some of the most influential, successful, and creative people in the world have had bipolar. There is sufficient evidence that suggests that Vincent van Gogh, Ernest Hemingway, and Winston Churchill had bipolar disorder. Contemporary celebrities such as Catherine Zeta-Jones, Demi Lovato, and Carrie Fisher have spoken openly about their bipolar disorder. Artists and politicians, inventors and change agents, mothers and fathers, sisters and brothers, and up to 5 percent of the entire US population have bipolar!

Little did I know then that Michael would extend his commitment to treating those with bipolar as well as their families. That's why he has created this practical guide, which normalizes and destigmatizes a highly treatable psychiatric condition. In addition, Michael has already launched the Bipolar Network, an online community for patients and families with bipolar disorder, showing that his determination and commitment to help those in need hasn't stopped.

I was delighted and honored when Michael asked me to write the foreword to this extremely important and timely book. The fact you're reading this indicates your interest in bipolar. Perhaps you know someone. Or you treat someone. Or you are that someone.

Whatever your situation, this book will help you know how to *own* bipolar instead of having bipolar own you.

In this book, Michael teaches the reader what bipolar is, how to recognize it and how to treat it so you can live the remarkable, productive life that's within your reach. He makes accessible state-of-the-art neuroscience and basic brain functioning, while exploring causes that influence the emergence of bipolar. He takes you through the diagnosis and explains why the condition can be so difficult to accept. He explores medications such as lithium, lamotrigine, and the complex mix of mood stabilizers, antipsychotics, antidepressants, and anxiolytics that could be needed to medically treat bipolar. And he takes you into the hospitals and back into the community, emphasizing the critical need for family and social understanding and support.

Many people are reluctant to take medications because they think it means they are broken—that there's something wrong with them. In response, I tell them the Dr. Shrand view of medicine. First, I ask, "If you have a mountain to climb, will you do it in your bare feet? Of course not. To climb a mountain, you need the right equipment, and it doesn't matter how much." Medicine is simply equipment; it does not define *you*. And medication is just a part of the treatment; it isn't your *only* piece of equipment. To climb that mountain, you also need family, friends, work, music, sports, religion, medicine, therapy, school, art—and this book!

I also tell patients they *will* stabilize one day, but the medications may be complicated. As a way of foreshadowing, I say, "There will be a morning when you wake up and declare you're doing great and don't need to take your medicine. After all, you're feeling great. On that day, take your medicine. It's probably *because* of that equipment that you *are* doing great." It's part of owning bipolar.

Beyond taking medication, Michael offers a critical three-phase approach to therapy. *Owning Bipolar* leads you through the *pre-stabilization, stabilization,* and *post-stabilization* phases—each important in the ongoing treatment of the condition. Ultimately, the most important phase is to *own* having this condition. Acceptance can be a difficult struggle, often using the psychological defense of denial. "Not me!" or "Not my kid!"

In part, denial is an avoidance and a fear of being stigmatized. Who wants to say they have bipolar disorder? Even using terms such as "disorder" or "illness" can place a person at risk of being seen as unpredictable and therefore not trustworthy. Unfortunately, the innocent use of such words can unwittingly perpetuate the stigma around mental illness, lumping people into two groups: the *normal* and the *sick*. To accept and own bipolar, recognize that having this condition doesn't mean seeing *yourself* as broken or disordered, damaged or inferior. You do the best you can, now and always, as you respond to the environment around and within you. Having bipolar is not a death sentence, but a responsibility. Perhaps your emotions swing from manic and euphoric, even delusional and psychotic, to the very depths of depression and despair, even a desire to die. Still, you're in control! To take control of those mood swings is to accept you have this condition. This becomes easier when you fully embrace *who you are* at any moment—whether you're hungry or cranky, falling in love, or learning to trust.

Owning Bipolar teaches you how both patients and families can take control of this lifelong mental illness.

Once when I was working at a locked inpatient psychiatric hospital, the ambulance brought in a man I will call Mr. B. whom I had admitted multiple times for being depressed or manic. When I saw him in his room, Mr. B. sat in front of me, unkempt and unshaved, his hair a bramble. He'd been admitted almost six months before after being pulled over by a police officer for careening off a steel barrier on the state highway. This time, Mr. B. had been driving over 80 miles per hour *with his eyes closed.*

In his hospital room, Mr. B. got up, paced the floor, and then sat down and fidgeted—his body a mirror of the thoughts racing in his mind.

"What happened?" I asked. "Driving with your eyes closed at eighty? What were you thinking?"

Alternating between sitting, standing, and pacing, he simply said, "I'm God."

"God?" I asked.

"I'm God."

I knew if I challenged this delusion, I'd be incorporated into it somehow. Instead, I found myself saying, "God! That's an enormous responsibility, isn't it?"

His voice breathy with a sense of overwhelming appreciation, Mr. B. looked at me and said, "It is! I can't stand it anymore. I have to go back on my lithium!"

At that moment, Mr. B. took ownership of his bipolar and the equipment needed for his journey. My guess is, if he'd read this book, it might not have taken him so long.

On behalf of all the readers who will benefit, I want to thank Michael for writing this book. It is very much worth owning.

—Joseph Shrand, MD

JOSEPH SHRAND is an instructor of Psychiatry at the Harvard Medical School, medical director of CASTLE (Clean and Sober Teens Living Empowered), and chief of Child and Adolescent Psychiatry at the High Point Treatment Center in Brockton, Massachusetts.

Preface

· · · · · ·

A TEENAGE BOY SAT CALMLY on the couch in front of me recounting tales of vicious mood swings, drug use, and arm-cutting while his mother sat pensively next to him, her gaze off into the distance. His eye contact impressed me; most of his peers would not do as well under the circumstances. The boy expressed himself with surprising clarity, avoiding casual slang for well-versed ideas and appropriate clinical terminology to explain his raucous behavior. His level of awareness exceeded his years. I was intrigued.

"Where did you learn to talk about your problems like that?" I asked, early into our first meeting.

"In the hospital," he said confidently. "I learned a lot from the groups."

"That's great. So, what was the most important thing you learned?"

"I figured this out: If I just keep taking my medication, I'll be all right."

His mother's head gently pivoted, and then she looked at him. Her eyes welled with tears.

It caught my attention, and I commented, "You must be proud of him."

Crying a little more, she replied, "Yes, I'm proud of him." She reached for her son's hand and squeezed it softly. "I'm proud—

and terrified. He did great in the hospital, but I don't know what's supposed to happen next. Patients get to learn all about their problems. What about the family?"

"What *do* you know about his problems?" I asked.

Her tears retreated for a moment. "They told me he has bipolar disorder. They told me he needed to be on medication and would need to stay on it. They were great, but he's in my hands now. I read some stuff online, but I really don't know what bipolar disorder is all about."

She leaned toward me and asked earnestly, "Where do the families go to get help for bipolar disorder?"

I told her I would provide all the pertinent information about her son's condition while I continued the therapy started in the hospital. I would also guide her to additional resources that would increase her knowledge of the disorder.

She appeared grateful. "That's good," she responded. But I got the sense that was hardly good enough.

"Sounds like you need more than just information. You need lots of support, too."

"Yes," she exclaimed as tears coursed down her cheeks. Then her agony gushed out along with her tears. She opened up with her own stories of helplessly watching her son swing from uncontrollable mania to suicidal depression. "Sure, he's doing well on medications now, but what if he gives up prescribed medicine for addictive drugs? Or what if he's looking joyful, happy, and fine only to turn up dead one day?" All her nightmares flooded out. Then she admitted, "I don't know if I can do this all by myself."

It became obvious this mother wasn't convinced that her son's bipolar disorder was under real control. Getting him on meds wasn't enough, even though he expressed a clear understanding of that need. There was something more in her declaration that his journey into bipolar had a long way to go. And her journey was lagging behind.

Although the boy and I proceeded with psychotherapy for bipolar disorder (and his knowledge and enthusiasm really did pay off), it was his mother who stood out prominently in my mind. As individual psychotherapy progressed for her son, this mom also improved through her involvement in family sessions. It gave her an opportunity to express her fears openly and work through the pain of her son's untreated mood swings. It reinforced the idea she was not alone in her parenting. But she never stopped talking about what she saw as the lack of support for bipolar patients and their families. She was convinced she couldn't do it all by herself—because no one really can.

And yet, for bipolar patients and families everywhere, that appears to be the subtle expectation. I believe that's due to crucial deficits in how we as a society have approached bipolar disorder.

The image of that mom leaning in, relating something vital for me, and repeating it several times was an urgent call to action. I reflected on my own training in psychotherapy and what I actually knew about bipolar. It became clearer this prevalent mood disorder, once known as manic depression, isn't well understood. How many patients and their families are left without sufficient knowledge and support for managing a lifelong mental illness?

After discussions with professional colleagues and people affected by bipolar, I began developing a dual clinical and educational program for bipolar patients and their loved ones in my community of Denver, Colorado. During the research for this effort, I discovered that nearly two-thirds of all bipolar patients are initially diagnosed with a different mental illness. The literature consistently reflected a fundamental clinical problem with bipolar disorder: *It often is misunderstood, misidentified, and mistreated.*

As a result, patients needlessly suffer the effects of mood swings—often for many years—and their families frequently are without a clear direction about what to do. To personalize these issues, I established the website BipolarNetwork.com and asked people who are confronting bipolar every day to submit their stories and share their struggles.

What I heard from those submissions—and from people attending the community education groups, as well as from new patients in my practice—affirmed what the research told me. And it confirmed what that one mother had stressed to me. *Bipolar patients and families often feel lost in the mental-health-system process.*

Despite the many excellent mental health clinicians available, the diagnosis and treatment of this lifelong mental illness lacks a unified method as well as a set of expectations for patients and families to rally around. Instead, they often fall through the cracks of a cumbersome mental health system that moves in many directions with vastly different standards. That is why I believe it is absolutely necessary for patients and families to understand what bipolar is, where it comes from, how to treat both the disorder itself as well as the lasting damage created by mood swings. Most important, that responsibility has to be shared before and during the main junctures of bipolar treatment, then later while sustaining one's mental and relational well-being.

Increasingly, the practice of modern medicine is about patients taking greater responsibility for their own health care. Mental health should be no different. *Owning Bipolar* is about taking responsibility for understanding, accepting, and treating a lifelong mental illness. As the title states, it's about how to "own" bipolar in your life.

Nobody Is at Fault

HAVING BIPOLAR DISORDER IS NOT your fault.

You didn't cause this to happen because you have been a bad person, or bad parent, or bad spouse, or bad daughter or son, or anything bad at all. You couldn't have done anything different to stop the inevitable formulation of this problem. It was foisted on you without your permission.

If you are a parent or family member of someone diagnosed with bipolar disorder, you aren't at fault either. You didn't do something wrong while you were pregnant. You didn't parent the wrong way, or discipline the wrong way, or do anything wrong at all.

Nobody is at fault for having this chronic, lifelong, genetic brain disease. Researchers have shown that up to 5 percent of the world's population has bipolar disorder.[1] Out of every twenty people you pass today, likely one of them has bipolar disorder. Many studies have found the main cause of bipolar disorder is genetic. That means what is coded in the genes of new human beings can dictate whether they'll be at risk of developing bipolar disorder

1

later in life. No one can change their genes, which are the basic building blocks of a person's biology. That's why having bipolar is nobody's fault.

When a person has the genetic makeup for bipolar, many possible internal or external events can act as catalysts or "triggers" for the disorder. And they can be numerous—from moderate emotional conflicts in daily life to severe losses or psychological trauma. At times, bipolar disorder surfaces when someone has a hormonal shift, such as after giving birth or while navigating adolescence. Bipolar also can emerge because of the severe stress over an important change in life, such as the loss of a job, relationship breakup, or health impairments. Substance abuse is often a big catalyst. Being away from home for the first time in life can create too many stressors, producing the first signs of bipolar. Many of these life events are unavoidable; some may be preventable. But just because bipolar can run in families, doesn't mean that family members' decisions or actions caused bipolar disorder.

Any number of factors can trigger symptoms. But one thing is true: *Once bipolar disorder is accurately diagnosed and treated, it's a highly manageable disease that can be controlled throughout the patient's lifetime.*

That last part sounds easy, doesn't it? So why read this book?

Because getting from the first sign of mood swings to a bipolar treatment program can be a long, complicated, and painful process. And even then, progressing from treatment to long-term disease management can be even more tedious. Bipolar disorder can announce itself in multiple ways and yet conceal itself in stealthy ways, too. In this book, I'll show you why bipolar is difficult to recognize, and provide clearer ways to identify it, so we can get to a proper bipolar treatment plan right away.

Unfortunately, studies have shown what I believe to be a problem for so many bipolar patients and their families: From the first time a bipolar-type mood event occurs to the first time bipolar disorder is specifically treated, a typical patient will have gone an average of nearly ten years without proper care.[2]

That's right—ten years! One question you may have is, "What are these people with bipolar doing all this time?" That question has different but equally disturbing answers. These people who have bipolar but don't know it or haven't been diagnosed are suffering with the consequences of untreated mood swings. However, it's not simply because they're avoiding getting help. On average, people with bipolar consult about four mental health professionals before they're accurately diagnosed with the disorder, while almost two-thirds will have been misdiagnosed at least once.[3] More often than not, professionals diagnose other psychological conditions, some of which may have similar symptoms, such as major depression and ADHD, but miss the bigger overall problem—bipolar disorder mood swings. That doesn't mean mental health professionals don't know what they're doing. I believe in mental health practice and recommend getting professional consultations throughout this book. But as you'll see, many complications can get in the way of identifying and treating bipolar disorder. Patients and families need information *and a solid plan* to collaborate with treatment professionals for ultimate success. Without a firm grasp of what it takes to *own* bipolar, people seeking help can fall through the cracks of the mental health system.

The Difficulty of Diagnosis

Along with difficulties in recognizing bipolar mood swings, another important issue of delayed treatment is something commonly called denial. This defense method can be present in patients, but also in family members who have difficulty understanding or accepting the reality of bipolar in their lives. For many patients, the idea of forever giving up mania is a tough pill to swallow, because they may have enjoyed the great feelings of energy and hypercreativity that come with a manic episode, and how those feelings can provide relief from depression. For family members, knowing that bipolar disorder will be around for a long

The Specter of Suicide

One fact is worthy of serious and urgent consideration: *Suicide is prevalent in bipolar disorder.* Suicide potential is at least twenty times higher among people with bipolar compared to everyone else.[4] Remember all of those people with bipolar who had sought treatment—sometimes for years—and weren't properly diagnosed? No longer can we stick our heads in the sands of denial, misinformation, or fear because bipolar disorder is an extremely lethal mental illness. In 2014, more than 42,000 people in the United States died from suicide,[5] and it's believed that bipolar disorder may account for one-quarter of those suicides.[6] Can you imagine if foreign agents or terrorists killed 10,000 Americans every year? What do you think the national response would be?

We can't wait around for things to just get better on their own. We need to understand how devastating bipolar can be, and start *owning* it with courage.

---

time feels overwhelming. They may avoid confronting the problem of bipolar in their lives because of how unreasonable or angry their bipolar loved ones can become. Under the weight of so much perceived pressure, fear, and even misinformation, people often want to avoid accepting reality. But by not facing the truth, they risk losing health, finances, and trust in their relationships.

Owning Bipolar

You may be angry or confused by your "uncontrollable" mood swings. You may have experienced frustrations with the mental health system. You may be concerned about and scared for your loved one because you don't know what to do. But that's about to change. Many great thinkers through the ages have proclaimed,

"Knowledge is power." I agree with them. The fears and frustration and uncertainty of all that we don't understand—all of these— can be overcome with the real power of knowledge.

U.S. President Franklin D. Roosevelt said, "The only thing we have to fear is fear itself." He was convinced that fear was our only true enemy, and he held that conviction despite all the terrible forces gaining command in the world around him. Experiencing fear is part of being human. But it's truly our only enemy—the only thing to fear even in the face of bipolar disorder.

And what do people fear most? They fear what they don't understand and refuse to trust. Yet with the power of knowledge, fear retreats into its cowardly little hole, back into the recesses of our expanded minds. Knowledge can overcome the anxieties of the great work ahead in treating this chronic mental illness.

Owning Bipolar can help you become an expert at your own illness—bipolar disorder. Yes, this is your illness, whether you're the patient or a relative of a patient. And it's a good time to own it. When bipolar first visited you, the disorder called the shots. It made decisions for you; it ran your life. It drove your car too fast, burned your bank account, drunk-dialed, and then cursed all the wrong people. It pushed hard to violate commitments, teasing an otherwise intelligent person into a delusion of life without consequences. It believed without question that a bulletproof, free-of-responsibility, immortal existence was within reach. But then, after riding high, it dumped you into a pit of despair, desperation, and perhaps even suicidal feelings or actions. No more!

Owning Bipolar exposes bipolar, and by doing so it takes away its manipulative authority. It breaks bipolar down into understandable parts so you know what to expect from diagnosis, treatment, and long-term management. You'll learn what patients and family members need to know for themselves— individually, and together—and how to communicate specific needs to one another.

You can also share your new expertise with professionals whom you've hired to provide appropriate bipolar assessment and treatments. Instead of being a passive patient, you'll have the tools to discuss bipolar disorder and its treatment concerns in a fresh, empowered, and collaborative way.

"Owning" bipolar means this chronic mental illness is neither ignored nor feared completely. It calls for being unafraid of treatment and all the things people fear about being labeled "mentally ill." After learning she had bipolar disorder, a woman I know said, "Thank God! I thought I was going crazy!" To her, "crazy" didn't describe herself. "Crazy" meant something was happening to her that she didn't understand, and she feared no one else could understand it either. Instead of fearing the diagnosis, she found relief in understanding what she faced. Having options for treatment and support meant she wasn't alone in her newfound mission of owning bipolar.

If you're a bipolar patient or suspect you may have bipolar, you will benefit from the knowledge in these chapters along with a clearer understanding of what your loved ones are going through. That's not intended to make you feel worse than you already feel; rather, it provides an opportunity to address these problems with the people you care about the most.

If you aren't the person diagnosed with bipolar, *Owning Bipolar* is just as much for you as your loved one who has the illness. Family members believe they're steps behind their bipolar loved one and also feel disconnected from the treatment process. If you feel this way, this book can help you get caught up in your bipolar loved one's life.

To own bipolar and thus control it requires understanding as much as you can about it. You're setting out to own bipolar, so learn its history, its background, and its potential for the future. You take so much care in buying a car, learning its history, driving it around, listening and feeling for the slightest imperfections. You want to know exactly what to expect before owning it. Take even more effort to know bipolar because you'll own it for a long time to come. This book puts you in the driver's seat.

Notes

1. Drancourt, N., Etain, B., Lajnef, M., Henry, C., Raust, A., Cochet. B., et al. (2012). Duration of untreated bipolar disorder: Missed opportunities on the long road to optimal treatment. *Acta Psychiatrica Scandinavica, 127*(2), 136–144.
2. Ibid.
3. Hirschfeld, R. M., Lewis, L., & Vornik, L. A. (2003). Perceptions and impact of bipolar disorder: How far have we really come? Results of the National Depressive and Manic-Depressive Association 200 survey of individuals with bipolar disorder. *Journal of Clinical Psychiatry, 64*(2), 161–174.
4. Berk, M., Scott, J., Macmillan, I., Callaly, T., & Christensen, H. M. (2013). The need for specialist services for serious and recurrent mood disorders. *Australian & New Zealand Journal of Psychiatry, 47*(9), 815–818.
5. Drapeau, C. W., & McIntosh, J. L. (for the American Association of Suicidology). (2015). U.S.A. *suicide 2014: Official final data.* Washington, DC: American Association of Suicidology. Retrieved from http://www.suicidology.org
6. American Psychiatric Association. (2013). *Diagnostic and statistical manual of mental disorders* (5th ed.). Washington, DC: Author, 131.

CHAPTER 1

· · · · · ·

Origins of Bipolar Disorder

BIPOLAR DISORDER HAS BEEN KNOWN as manic depression and by other names throughout history. Descriptions of the cycling of "genius" and "madness" along with "melancholia" date back to ancient Greece. During the Middle Ages, much of what was believed about psychological disorders came from myths, legends, and falsehoods. Bipolar disorder and other mental illnesses were feared because they were misunderstood. As a result, many people were often viewed as outcasts, rather than human beings who suffered ailments requiring specific treatments, along with compassion from others. By the nineteenth century, some physicians wanted to take mania and depression out of the dark ages of mental illness and catalog bipolar-type symptoms so they could be treated like other medical diseases, but disagreement about what causes bipolar and how to treat it continued throughout the twentieth century.[1] Not until recently has bipolar disorder been widely accepted as having biological, genetic causes.

Today the term "bipolar disorder" refers to a class of psychiatric disorders involving severe episodes of contrasting mood states. "Bipolar" literally means "two poles." Just as the North Pole and South Pole represent the farthest points on the globe, bipolar mood swings span the length of the emotional spectrum. Although many people experience mood swings throughout their lives for various reasons, bipolar disorder is distinct in that the cycles of both mania and depression can present destructive consequences to the individual's health and well-being.

What causes bipolar disorder? Although it is called a mental disorder, the foundations of bipolar are genetic, which is the strongest and most consistent factor for the disease.[2] Without this genetic factor, bipolar disorder would likely not exist in any particular individual. Moreover, it is believed that bipolar is caused by underlying problems with brain development and/or brain circuitry. Some researchers who study stem cells—the basic building blocks that form specialized cells in our bodies—note that stem cells in people with bipolar develop differently than those without bipolar.[3] Other researchers who observe brain functioning believe that in people with bipolar disorder the parts of their neurology that typically regulate emotions are not well designed. Two of those brain areas are likely the *prefrontal cortex* or *PFC* and the *amygdala* (pronounced ah-MIG-dah-lah).[4]

The PFC, located in the front of the brain, gives humans the ability to form and use logic. It's in charge of understanding consequences and anticipating future events based on experience. The PFC learns right from wrong and helps us think in a rational, organized, and socially appropriate way. It sometimes is referred to as the "newest" part of the brain because as humans evolved, the PFC likely was refined through living in organized social groups and civilization itself. It's often credited with giving us a sense of self-awareness or consciousness about who we are and what our purpose should be in life.

We also refer to PFC activity as "executive functioning." Compare it to the top executive of a company making the hardest, most complicated decisions and then passing instructions down to the workers. The workers carry out the plans and send feedback to the executive who then makes further decisions. And so it goes in our brains. The PFC acts as the top executive while other brain structures carry out orders and give feedback.

The amygdala lies deep in the central region of the brain and is involved in producing emotions and processing emotional memories. During human evolution, the amygdala was likely well in place as the PFC was developing. While the PFC is more thoughtful, the amygdala is more reactive.

Emotional memories often include those deep within that have formed over many years and even memories that are repressed or unconscious. The amygdala alerts the executive that a current situation resembles things—real or imagined—from an old or repressed memory. That is why someone reacts in fear to something that is not inherently frightening: not necessarily because it's a real threat, but because it resembles one. Or it may explain why someone falls quickly and madly in love with another person. It's not always because this person is worthy of it, but because of a deeper emotional memory that this person elicits.

In a person with bipolar, the functions of the PFC and amygdala, and how they communicate with each other, don't work in the kind of balanced and consistent way necessary for normal functioning—at least not all the time.

If the parts of the brain responsible for emotion and logic don't work well together, what could happen? Without balanced and harmonious interactions between those parts, you might expect big fluctuations in mood states that are inadequately limited by logical thoughts or moral beliefs. For example, the amygdala may alert the rest of the brain to some potential consequence in a sudden burst of emotion and physical reactions, like increased heart rate and muscle tension. It puts the body in a state of readiness for action. But the PFC uses logic and reason to assess the real extent of the potential danger and the best way to handle the situation. If a person with bipolar is in a manic zone and feeling euphoric, the PFC may be blunted and not in sync with the amygdala's signals. As a result, the person either may ignore the possible danger of the consequence, or feel so good that he or she interprets the distress signal the wrong way and believes that this experience isn't dangerous at all! In fact, the person may view it as fun, or a sign that he or she is impervious to such a danger.

Along with shifting brain patterns lacking proper regulation between the PFC and the amygdala, measurable shifts in brain chemicals occur during mood swings, changing how nerve cells communicate with each other. These chemicals are called neurotransmitters because they allow chemical messages to transmit from nerve cell to nerve cell. One neurotransmitter is dopamine, which in the right amount produces a sense of pleasure, and helps provide a "reward" when we are learning something, or need a sense of motivation. Another neurotransmitter is serotonin, which in the proper concentration, prevents depression and aids in overall mood stability. Problems in mood regulation occur if there is too much or too little serotonin in the brain. Likewise, serious problems can occur when there is too much or too little dopamine, including possible psychotic symptoms.

This helps explain what people with bipolar experience. Perhaps you can now appreciate why bipolar patients can't simply stop their mood swings through sheer will. People can't just close their eyes, grit their teeth, and make their brains do something they were not designed to do. But understanding the brain should help in considering the needs of people with bipolar and can help us act more compassionately toward reworking some of these faulty brain functions.

Causes of Bipolar Disorder

There are two groups of causes:

1. Predispositional
2. Catalytic

Predispositional causes involve genetics and faulty brain development with respect to mood regulation. Catalytic causes, or catalysts, include all other factors outside or inside the body that switch on the actual mood swing from one extreme to another.

Predispositional Causes

Bipolar disorder is passed through family genetics and appears to affect how the brain is formed to handle mood regulation. When someone has a gene that likely can produce a certain medical disorder, scientists may say the person has a "predisposition" for that disorder. When I evaluate new patients, I ask about their family's mental health histories to understand whether they may be predisposed to bipolar disorder. If anyone in the family tree, particularly the closest genetic relatives, experienced mood swings, I know they could be predisposed to bipolar. I then make precise inquiries into their backgrounds, especially where bipolar symptoms may have been hiding in their own life history.

For example, did Mom or Dad show signs of mood swings? High levels of irritability followed by deep sadness? What about Grandma or Grandpa? Were there stories of erratic behavior? Were there aunts or uncles who had serious bouts of depression or psychotic symptoms? Did anyone need serious psychiatric care? Suffer from addictions? What happened to these family members? A little detective work may be useful to figure out a genetic history of bipolar. Such information should be given to a mental health professional ahead of any bipolar-disorder evaluation.

Catalytic Causes

I refer to the many ways bipolar is triggered as manic catalysts. Why do I say "manic" catalysts and not "bipolar" catalysts? Because many people have periods of severe depression before they have mania. Depressive episodes can be triggered, too, but mania (and hypomania in Bipolar II) defines bipolar disorder separately from major depression alone.

Let's look at some manic catalysts. As people mature, their brains have to find a way to deal with various stressors and challenges. The rigors of developing into an adult and all the added responsibilities could build into manic catalysts. Depression and anxiety may be present at any point in life, but often the specific symptoms of bipolar disorder emerge in adolescence or early adulthood.

Another catalyst for mania can be related to hormonal changes. These are certainly expected for any adolescent bipolar patient, but they also explain why some women with postpartum hormonal changes begin to develop bipolar symptoms if they are predisposed to bipolar. In fact, a presentation of mental illness in the early postpartum phase is an indicator for possible bipolar disorder.[5] Other internal factors in a person's changing physiology, including thyroid problems and other medical conditions, can be catalysts for mania.

A critical manic catalyst is substance abuse. You may wonder whether it would be considered an *internal* catalyst because the chemical inside the body affects the brain, or an *external* one because the individual is compelled to ingest the substance. It's both. In addition, substance abuse often involves its own variety of external cues, such as social events or stressors. The brain of an addicted person also provides its own triggers to ingest more of the drug. It's important to remember that not only can substances lift bipolar symptoms out of hiding, they also can be used to "self-medicate" those symptoms, especially when the user is depressed. Self-medication means the person abusing substances isn't just trying to get high, but is really trying to improve his or her bipolar symptoms to feel better—even if he or she does not recognize this as the real reason for using those drugs. I will discuss later how this idea fits in to treating people who have both bipolar disorder and a substance abuse problem.

I'm frequently asked about the role of psychological trauma in triggering mania and bipolar in general. If a person has struggled with traumatic experiences now or in the past, symptoms can form sooner and/or more severely. Traumatic experiences are extraordinary and terrible events that either happened directly to us or we witnessed. Trauma certainly can result in many different and severe mental disorders; however, I'm convinced these catalysts would require having a predisposition for bipolar to form the disorder in the chronic, lifelong pattern we know.

To summarize, bipolar is genetic in its foundations, but life events can act as catalysts that arouse symptoms or make them worse.

Types of Bipolar Disorder

Bipolar disorder has three basic types:

1. Bipolar I Disorder
2. Bipolar II Disorder
3. Cyclothymia

Bipolar I is marked by severe manic episodes, what many call "full-blown" mania. Although Bipolar I may be easier to diagnose than the other types, it's often harder to treat over the course of the illness. Someone with Bipolar I will suffer longer or sometimes more intense episodes of mania than other types and therefore will experience more consequences. Some instances of Bipolar I include psychotic symptoms, such as hallucinations or severely delusional thinking. More opportunities are available for treatment of Bipolar I because severe levels of the disorder tend to get more attention. However, consistent participation in care is difficult to sustain, because the consequences of Bipolar I can injure personal resources—such as financial and social supports—and thus make the ability to avoid symptom relapses more difficult. Bipolar I can emerge anytime, but the average age of onset is about 18 years old.[6]

Bipolar II is marked by manic episodes of shorter duration and sometimes with less intensity, known as hypomania (which literally means "under mania"). The same manic symptoms as in Bipolar I might exist, but the hypomanic episodes tend to last at least four days instead of seven days as in Bipolar I. Thus, it can do somewhat less damage to the individual's life, at least in the shorter term. Bipolar I had generally been considered the worst form of bipolar, but that assessment is changing. That's because the depressive episodes of Bipolar II can be just as severe—or even worse—than depressive episodes in Bipolar I. Moreover, those with hypomanic episodes are harder to diagnose. Hypomanic episodes may be viewed as symptomatic of active people too stressed out by life, or people who have another kind of mental health problem such as anxiety or a personality disorder. Bipolar II patients tend to be somewhat older than Bipolar I patients, with an average age of onset in the mid-20s,[7] so hypomania could be confused with a hard-driving, young adult lifestyle. And because Bipolar II patients tend to be highly productive and more "functional" than Bipolar I patients, they may not consider mood regulation to their benefit. People around the Bipolar II person would tend to disagree. A hypomanic episode indicates a definite change in the person's behavior compared with when hypomania or depression is not present. Daily life functioning is impaired as a result, including mismanagement of responsibilities in one's job or school, and a decline in health, finances, and relationships. Bipolar II may be somewhat easier to treat, but it can be more difficult to identify and diagnose adequately.

Cyclothymia literally means "cycling emotions." This form of bipolar is marked by less severe but more frequent changes in mood than other kinds of bipolar disorder. It forms a chronic, consistent pattern that lasts at least two years in adults and one year in children. The mood episodes are very compact in time. A person with cyclothymia can go from extremely excited and

There are other forms of bipolar disorder induced strictly by substance use or certain medical disorders that may not have underlying genetic, predispositional causes. Mood swings unrelated to bipolar disorder can occur as the result of certain brain traumas or thyroid conditions. If you have any history of these medical disorders, or past or current substance use, be sure to inform your treatment professional to get the most accurate diagnosis for your situation.

"happy" to sad, anxious, and tearful in a matter of a day or two, or even just a few hours. For people in the earliest stages of bipolar, it is not unusual to show a cyclothymic or "rapid cycling" pattern. This is observed as a "prodromal" form of the disease, which means the full disorder has not yet presented itself. This happens commonly with adolescent patients in particular. When a young patient shows symptoms of cyclothymia, seek immediate evaluation and possibly treatment. Although that mood pattern might diminish, it could be a sign of something worse to come.

In addition to these three basic types, more variations of bipolar disorder help treatment professionals refine their diagnoses. But understanding these basics will assist you in becoming an expert of your own illness.

Notes

1. Fieve, R. R. (1997). *Moodswing* (2nd ed.). New York: Bantam Books, 29–56.
2. American Psychiatric Association. (2013). *Diagnostic and statistical manual of mental disorders* (5th ed.). Washington, DC: Author, 130.
3. Fox, M. (2014, March 25). Stem cells shed light on bipolar disorder. NBC News. Retrieved November 11, 2014, from http://www.nbcnews.com/health/health-news/stem-cells-shed-light-bipolar-disorder-n61731

4. Townsend, J., & Altshuler, L. L. (2012). Emotion processing and regulation in bipolar disorder: A review. *Bipolar Disorders, 14*(4), 326–339.
5. Munk-Olsen, T., Laursen, T. M., Meltzer-Brody, S., Mortensen, P. B., & Jones, I. (2012). Psychiatric disorders with postpartum onset: Possible early manifestations of bipolar affective disorders. *Archives of General Psychiatry, 69*(4), 428–434.
6. American Psychiatric Association. *Diagnostic and statistical manual,* 130.
7. Ibid. 137.

CHAPTER 2

Diagnosing Bipolar Mania, Hypomania, Depression

MUCH OF WHAT'S USED TO DIAGNOSE bipolar disorder comes from the fifth edition of *Diagnostic and Statistical Manual of Mental Disorders* (DSM-5; 2013). This vital guide for mental health professionals contains lots of technical information. So you don't have to wade through this tome, I will provide you some of the key clinical information from the DSM-5 as it pertains to the person with bipolar. But I will also provide additional concepts to better identify and understand how bipolar presents in daily life.

Diagnosing Mania

The term "mania" is used to describe a particular mood state associated with Bipolar I. However, mania also generically describes a range of manic mood zones that include mania and psychotic mania in Bipolar I (psychotic features include hallucinations, such as hearing "voices," or delusions, which are thoughts that are far outside of reality) and hypomania in

Bipolar II (typically shorter in duration and with a lesser degree of consequences than mania).

Generally, the manic person's mood can be described as abnormally elevated, euphoric, or expansive (unrestrained), or it can be dysphoric (irritable and agitated). Essentially, the mood state in mania can make people look like they're on a mind-altering drug that makes them appear "high" or "cranked." However, to correctly diagnose a manic episode, it has to be made clear it isn't a direct consequence of drug use or another medical or psychiatric problem.

During the period of the manic mood state, three or more of the following must be present (or four if the mania is dysphoric [irritable], and not euphoric):

- **Inflated self-esteem or grandiosity.** Individuals in a manic episode often see themselves as more special than the people around them. They may suddenly view themselves as incapable of defeat or free from negative consequences, as if they are "bulletproof" in the world. They often feel as if they're the king or queen of all they survey. This is known as "euphoric mania."

  Manic individuals also can believe they have a special purpose or message to send to the world. They may indeed be talented, but while manic they exaggerate the importance of their projects or ideas. Some manic individuals, however, aren't quite as talented as their mania leads them to believe. Their grandiosity allows them to create wonderfully imaginative scenarios for their success, but they lack the skills, discipline, or basic sense of reality to bring those ideas to fruition.

  When psychotic features are present, grandiosity reaches a high level of intensity, and is ultimately marked by hallucinations and delusional beliefs that far exceed reality. Patients may see themselves as messengers from God or lose touch with their sense of mortality, as if their "divine mission" will protect them from any and all harm against them. They may hear voices telling them of their greatness or saying how no one else can understand them. Delusional beliefs become so compelling that patients may abandon their adult responsibilities to pursue whatever the unreal beliefs or hallucinations may dictate. In some cases, these individuals may be found away from home, following what they're "told to do," but with a bizarre sense of elation in every misbegotten step they take.

With or without psychotic features, a person with inflated self-esteem or grandiosity can experience feelings of sharpened focus, fulfillment of life purpose, or an overwhelming sense of understanding life's ultimate meaning. The intense pleasure from these amazing feelings can lead people with bipolar to "protect" their mania through various degrees of denial, even when it's accompanied by less agreeable symptoms.

- **Decreased need for sleep.** This differs from insomnia. Insomnia is when people have bouts of sleeplessness when they've tried different ways to fall asleep and/or are awakened when they didn't want to be. That isn't the same as having a decreased need for sleep.

Unlike people with insomnia, manic people do not *want* to sleep. Instead, they desire to keep going with various tasks—some productive, some unproductive, and some ultimately destructive. Artists, composers, inventors, entrepreneurs, and entertainers who have mania often work themselves to exhaustion, but not until their manic phase ends. Even so, they frequently defend their lack of sleep by saying, "I don't need it. I feel great if I get just two hours!" Or, "Sure it's three in the morning, but I'm ready to go, so I'm off for a run!"

This symptom of bipolar mania rarely gets the attention it deserves. That's because in no other mental disorder do people embrace and defend their lack of sleep with such vigor. Non-manic people who work late hours typically won't say how great they feel the next day. They often characterize their lack of sleep as a short-term necessity, but they look forward to sleeping long hours later to compensate. By comparison, manic people rarely look forward to downtime. Their mania is characterized by persistent energy and drive. Besides, for them, downtime may be depression.

• **More talkative than usual, pressured speech, or pressure to keep talking.** Manic people can be delightful, charming, charismatic, annoying, bizarre, or even scary when attempting to communicate with others. They're typically difficult to interrupt and can be tangential; that is, they can go on about different subjects as if they're authorities on each. They don't speak concisely.

Perhaps you've witnessed a serious car accident and called 911. If you were upset and anxious, you probably wanted to relay all the information to the dispatcher as quickly as possible. In that urgent situation, your speech could be described as "pressured." Manic people often talk this way, even in otherwise calm circumstances. Pressured speech reflects their constant sense of urgency and can mobilize others who follow them. Or it can position the person as the "boy who cried wolf"—always talking as if something big is going to happen, but that something never materializes.

• **Flight of ideas or racing thoughts.** Manic people can go on and on with varied and fragmented thoughts, often being in a state of hypercreativity. However, the constant barrage of thoughts can be both overwhelming and disturbing, with the difference relating to the type of mania they're experiencing.

With euphoric mania, individuals revel in their thoughts, often believing they can formulate new, powerful theories or wildly exciting accomplishments. With dysphoric mania, they can become frustrated with their own madness or with how others get "turned off" by their rants.

Manic people often begin their manic episode feeling euphoric, but eventually they become dysphoric toward the end. Why? Because the world around them presents perceived barriers to their sense of greatness. Imagine having amazing thoughts about inventing wonderful things and solving complex problems, only to have others dismiss them as "nuts." In a personal exchange, dysphoric mania often sounds like this: "You just don't get it, do you? You just don't get it!"

- **Increase in goal-directed activity or psychomotor agitation.** This, in effect, separates manic *thoughts* and *speech* from manic *behavior*. Manic people can create intense and complex social situations entangling others in the process. They can become hyperactive or overextend on their various responsibilities. They can enact poorly planned ideas that ultimately sabotage social and occupational achievements. They can also pursue any number of radical and befuddling changes in physical appearance or affiliation (such as different social groups, political movements, religious beliefs, and so on).

Although this intense drive to get things done may sound appealing, such increases in activity can't be sustained. Too many "irons in the fire" means manic people frequently create more chaos than accomplishment. But when coupled with grandiosity, it becomes difficult to interrupt the manic person's goal-driven activities. What results? A path of destruction is left in the wake of the manic person's inflated sense of destiny.

Another hallmark of manic behavior is psychomotor agitation—a significant type of physical restlessness that includes muscle tension or anxiety. Pacing, hand wringing, and the inability to stay seated are examples of psychomotor agitation.

• **Distractibility.** No matter how great their ideas or goal-directed they seem, manic people can get easily distracted with unrelated activities in their environment. They also may become hyper-focused on a single thing, to the detriment of important tasks that actually need to be completed. You may wonder how a person in the throes of a manic episode can sustain any type of success, a job, or a relationship. Often, they can't. Their inability to complete projects or fulfill essential duties can make them seem unreliable and irresponsible. However, it is not uncommon for others in their life to "cover" for them and compensate for their failure to carry out certain tasks. Generally, bipolar patients who have greater personal resources can hire or barter with others to care for certain responsibilities. But there's always a strain on personal relationships. Often, a parent-child type of interaction develops in marriages, meaning the person with bipolar has an unhealthy dependence on the spouse to care for adult responsibilities.

• **Excessive involvement in pleasurable or risky behaviors that have a high potential for painful consequences.** This symptom of mania brings the greatest attention to the disorder and the need for treatment. Manic people often can go on buying sprees, invest impulsively, or gamble away their paychecks. They might go on alcohol or drug binges, or act out sexually through promiscuity or other indiscretions. They also might pursue potentially harmful acts to fulfill a need for an adrenaline rush. This includes driving at extreme speeds and other activities that could put themselves and others in great danger. Severe irritability can result in hostile or even violent behaviors against self or others.

No matter what pleasurable or risky behaviors manic people indulge in, there is no reasonable judgment or insight into the long-term effects of their decisions. The results of these actions could mean legal or medical emergencies, bankruptcy or homelessness, and most often, broken relationships. These are referred to as the "functional consequences" of bipolar disorder. For the families of people with bipolar, they're often called "the last straw."

Diagnosing Bipolar Depression

The depression end of the bipolar cycle can be more devastating than the manic side. Here, the mood is intensely sad, dark, and overpowering. A person with bipolar depression often experiences the painful functional consequences of the manic episode, and the previously inflated self-esteem has turned into shame and despair. Alcohol and drug abuse have turned away from a manic-style party toward self-medication. Suicidal thoughts, self-harm, or the potential to harm others are of great concern during this time.

When depressed people with bipolar are admitted to inpatient or outpatient treatment, their history of mania isn't always evident. They may be diagnosed initially with major depressive disorder. That misdiagnosis typically occurs when the patient is experiencing a major depressive episode but has no known history of mania or hypomania. When a depressed person is evaluated by a mental health professional, the clinician should know the patient's history. Precise treatment choices require a full history to know whether the patient is "coming down" from a manic episode—one that could be many days, months, or even years in the making. If the question isn't asked about mania or the patient fails to mention it or the patient doesn't realize what it is, a diagnosis of major depression is typically the only diagnosis made. This is important because certain medications for depression, when taken alone, could be a catalyst for a manic episode, thus worsening the entire condition.

Note: It is also useful for the clinician to know if a patient has a history of major depressive episodes to make an accurate bipolar diagnosis, especially if Bipolar II is suspected. A person with Bipolar I might have had major depressive episodes in the past, but that is not necessary for the diagnosis. However, in Bipolar II, the person must have at least one major depressive episode along with hypomania to have this diagnosis. That's because people who have occasional hypomanic episodes are not considered to have any type of mood disorder, including bipolar disorder. A person can have periods of hypomania and live a functional life. But when major depression has been present, the diagnosis is the mood disorder of Bipolar II.

Symptoms for a major depressive episode in bipolar disorder include at least five of the following over the same two-week period:

- Depressed mood for most of the day, nearly every day
- Diminished pleasure or interest in usual activities
- Significant change in appetite, or weight gain or loss
- Insomnia or hypersomnia (oversleeping)
- Psychomotor agitation or restlessness
- Fatigue or loss of energy
- Feelings of worthlessness, or excessive or inappropriate guilt
- Diminished ability to think or concentrate
- Recurrent thoughts of death, or suicidal thoughts or actions

Bipolar Mood Zones

Understanding all bipolar symptoms is vital in recognizing the disorder in its individual parts. This helps distinguish it from other psychological problems while isolating problem areas for the ensuing conversations about treatment. I have found, however, that people who work toward owning their own bipolar disorder appreciate knowing about the seven bipolar mood zones. They often cite these zones to better identify and explain their different mood episodes in the context of their day-to-day lives. From a clinical viewpoint, bipolar episodes come and go, sometimes giving the impression that bipolar disorder itself comes and goes, too. Understanding that people with bipolar live in various mood "zones"—and don't only contend with "episodes"—can help them think of bipolar disorder as a single, lifelong disease.

Seven Bipolar Mood Zones

The seven mood zones are listed from the top of the manic high to the bottom of the depressive low. The top three are considered the manic zones; the bottom three are the depressive zones.

Psychotic mania
Mania
Hypomania
Baseline
Dysthymia
Major depression
Psychotic depression

Psychotic Mania. Extreme bizarre behaviors mark this severe type of mania. Those who have it often experience periods of delusional thoughts and actions, and, at times, hallucinations.

Themes tend to be grandiose, but they can frighten others. The episode can be euphoric or dysphoric. The psychotic symptoms subside once the manic episode has ended.

During an episode, hospitalization can be required. Having one episode in a lifetime is enough to be diagnosed as Bipolar I, with psychotic features.

Mania. This mood zone lasts at least one week. It meets the criteria mentioned earlier and comes with severe consequences. The episode can be euphoric or dysphoric. Hospitalization may be needed. One episode in a lifetime is enough to be diagnosed as Bipolar I, but without psychosis.

Hypomania. This mood zone has the same features as mania but either is shorter in duration (minimum of four days) or has fewer severe consequences than in long episodes. Hypomania can be euphoric or dysphoric. The changes in behavior during this episode are regarded as out of character to those who know the hypomanic person. To be diagnosed as Bipolar II, they must have had at least one episode of major depression in their lifetime along with one episode of hypomania. Many people with hypomania can function adequately and with high productivity.

Baseline. This is the bipolar mood zone most people describe as "normal." But "normal" can mean different things to different people. Individuals can have different baseline zones, and even then their baseline may not feel like any particular type of emotion. It's mostly identified as the mid-range between the bipolar mood extremities.

Dysthymia. Pronounced dis-THIY-me-uh, this zone is best described as an episode of minor depression. It represents reduced mood (sadness, anxiety, and so on) below the person's baseline. Its depressive symptoms are less severe and last a shorter time than major depression.

Patients diagnosed with cyclothymia usually have episodes of dysthymia and hypomania that swing consistently over two years or more. If people have *occasional* periods of dysthymia and/or hypomania and have never met the criteria for Bipolar I or II, they don't have a bipolar disorder. Bipolar patients who are stabilized on medications sometimes experience occasional shifts between hypomania and dysthymia, but those mood changes tend to be connected to their current circumstances. This situation may actually represent a realistic emotional life pattern for some people.

Major Depression. An episode of at least two weeks of significant sadness, agitation, feelings of worthlessness, sleep and appetite impairments, reduced energy and activity, loss of ability to experience pleasure, and possible suicidal thoughts or actions mark this mood zone. Hospitalization might be needed depending on the extent of the depressive symptoms, but especially when suicidal intent is present.

Psychotic Depression. In this zone, severe major depression is marked by constant thoughts and/or actions around death or self-harm. Delusions and/or hallucinations often include dark, deprecating, or frightening themes. The psychotic symptoms subside once the depressive episode has ended. During the episode, however, hospitalization is often required.

ALTHOUGH THE SEVEN mood zones present various levels of bipolar symptoms, there isn't a single "safe zone" for anyone with untreated mood swings. It's important to consider that a person with bipolar could suffer related problems in any zone, including suicidal thoughts or actions. Patients and family members can look forward to returning to baseline as a respite from the chaos and anxiety of the other mood zones, but that isn't the time to rest. In fact, it may well be the best time to initiate action before the next turbulent mood event begins.

Evelyn's Story

Evelyn describes living in her manic zone this way:

> Mania actually is a high. You feel great. You're happy
> and creative. And everybody likes to be around you
> because you're the life of the party. My self-confidence
> is also at an all-time high. I feel like I am invincible.
> Sometimes that causes some problems.
>
> When I am in this state, I'll get into arguments be-
> cause I think I am right about everything, and then
> that'll make me agitated and angry. I get in such a
> state that I can't hear anything people around me are
> trying to say. But the highs are so amazing.
>
> But as amazing as they are, I'm starting to realize
> that the consequences aren't always so great. I want
> to be in this high, happy state, but I don't know if the
> consequences that come with it are worth it. Some-
> times I don't even see the consequences because I'm
> focused on being this great person and having a
> great time.[1]

Why Bipolar Disorder Is Difficult to Diagnose

Students of the mental health professions learn the importance
of what's called differential diagnosis. As practicing clinicians,
they spend their careers perfecting this skill. Differential diagnosis refers to the logical process necessary to separate one
mental disorder from another, especially when different disorders share certain symptoms. This is quite important with
bipolar disorder, which can be misdiagnosed or confused with
similar disorders.

Sets of symptoms—especially mania—in different disorders
can cross over with bipolar symptoms. It's good to know that

poorly regulated mood swings generally drive the symptoms of bipolar. When untreated mood swings subside or change, some or all of those symptoms also change. Bipolar symptoms are described as "episodic"—that is, they present in episodes that come and go over time. For disorders that get confused with bipolar disorder, the symptoms don't change through their course (until the symptoms are treated, of course). The symptoms of those disorders are "pervasive" in that they continue throughout the duration of the disorder.

The following common mental illnesses are often confused with bipolar disorder (and vice versa).

ADHD

Distractibility, agitation, increased activity, and hyper-focus are attributes usually found in both bipolar disorders and attention deficit hyperactivity disorder (ADHD). ADHD also has an "inattentive type" qualifier that applies to people who cannot consistently focus on topics in school or at work but show no significant signs of hyperactivity. However, they might exhibit anxiety that can be mistaken for bipolar-like agitation.

Bipolar and ADHD can exist together but are frequently confused for one another, especially in children. These children could also be suffering from a major depression or an anxiety disorder, but their agitation and excessive emotional upset can result in acting out behaviors that appear manic or hyperactive (as in ADHD). Generally, adults are easier to diagnose than teenagers for these and certain other mental disorders. It's best to work with a mental health professional or medical provider who specializes in children and teenagers, and has the expertise to differentiate among these problems.

One point of concern hinges on different treatment approaches. A primary treatment for ADHD involves medications known as "psychostimulants." Even though they stimulate certain aspects of brain functioning, psychostimulants in a person with

ADHD improve attention and focus, helping patients calm themselves. But caution must be used in treating ADHD when bipolar is suspected. Mood stabilization should occur first before adding psychostimulant medication specifically for ADHD.[2] That's because giving a psychostimulant without bipolar medications to someone with bipolar could be a catalyst for mania. If bipolar disorder is causing distractibility, treating the bipolar first will reduce the problem. At that point, ADHD can be reevaluated. If distractibility is alleviated, ADHD meds may be unnecessary. But if there is still some problem with attention that's not improving with bipolar treatment alone, then a psychostimulant may be helpful, without risk of increasing mania. That's why these two disorders require careful attention so a proper treatment plan doesn't put the patient at undue risk.

OCD

Obsessive-compulsive disorder (OCD) involves frequent and intrusive repetitive thoughts (obsessions) and/or behaviors (compulsions). Fundamentally, people with OCD attempt to stave off their intense anxiety or fears, which usually are irrational or unconscious. They eventually realize their recurring thoughts and actions are creating problems in their lives, but they can't stop OCD symptoms by using will alone. In time, the symptoms will overwhelm them.

People with entrenched, persistent compulsions can go about these behaviors in a ritualized way that requires considerable drive and energy. Thus, compulsive behaviors can appear to be manic in nature, particularly if the compulsions keep a person completely occupied day and night. Like major depression, OCD is frequently treated with antidepressant medications, which by themselves can induce mania in people who have bipolar disorder.

An important difference is that OCD behaviors are caused by internal fears with the primary purpose of staving off anxiety.

Bipolar mania is goal-oriented; that is, the behavior is driven to accomplish something—usually perceived to be something of great value, not simply avoiding anxiety.

Some people with bipolar disorder who are receiving proper treatment can look like they have OCD because they may be trying so hard to avoid a relapse of bipolar symptoms—especially depression—they appear "obsessed" with avoiding any potential triggers for those symptoms. This can happen in the early phases of bipolar treatment, when bipolar patients are accepting the disorder, and trying to avoid excessive feelings or missteps in daily life that could throw them back into mood swings. Acting overly cautious with bipolar is not a symptom of OCD. However, it requires further therapy to address a person's ongoing fears of returning to the symptoms of bipolar disorder.

Personality Disorders

Some personality disorders mimic signs of mania. At times, they're referred to as "characterological disorders" because they reflect severe, pervasive impairments in the individual's psychological or moral character. Borderline, narcissistic, and antisocial personality disorders can have some of the closest similarities to bipolar mania.

Borderline individuals typically display stark emotional changes, turbulent relationship patterns, and irresponsible or risky personal behaviors. A key component of borderline personality is called idealization/devaluation or "splitting."[3] This means a borderline person can idealize another person in a relationship (including a therapist during the course of therapy) as "all good" or a "perfect soul mate." Later, and usually without provocation, that same amazing person will be devalued as "all bad" or "useless."

These harsh instabilities in mood, relationships, and social behavior can appear manic. Any differentiation is complicated by the fact that those with borderline personality disorder can suffer severe depression with suicidal thoughts and actions in the same way people with bipolar can. But while the instability of mood is a constant problem with borderline personality, in bipolar, mood changes come and go with periods of baseline stability. People with borderline personality also intensely fear abandonment in relationships, which is not a feature of bipolar disorder.

Narcissistic personality disorder is marked by inflated self-esteem, grandiose self-regard, and unrealistic standards about love and achievement. Again, these features can appear to be manic, especially if narcissistic individuals are feeling frustrated. They often respond with high levels of irritability and anger. But in bipolar disorder, the inflated self-esteem and grandiosity decrease once the manic episode is over. People with narcissistic personality disorder have a constant need for admiration and a lack of empathy for others, and these features don't alter with changing moods.

Antisocial personality disorder includes not only severe impairments in relationships but also a callous disregard for rules, laws, and social norms. Antisocial personalities begin showing these disturbances during adolescence. Their behavior tends to be consistent, even if mood patterns change over time. Antisocial activity can result in constant run-ins with authority figures, the same way the irresponsible behaviors of manic individuals can cause clashes with authorities. How can the criminal justice system identify individuals who violate the law due to uncontrolled manic behavior but who would otherwise live as productive, law-abiding citizens?

This doesn't mean a bipolar disorder and a personality disorder can't coexist in the same person. But often one is mistaken for the other, resulting in delayed or ineffective treatment. Bipolar disorder is traditionally driven by episodic mood swings, and those drastic mood shifts do not by themselves reflect the total, pervasive character of a bipolar individual. When in baseline, the qualities of a bipolar individual are often different than the characteristics described in personality disorders.

Schizophrenia

The psychotic disorder of schizophrenia involves persistent delusional or disorganized thinking. It's frequently marked by hallucinations, mostly auditory ("hearing voices").

Delusions are false beliefs that reflect a complete absence of reality with wild, paranoid features. Some people with severe Bipolar I can experience similar schizophrenic-like symptoms during mood swings. The type of delusion in bipolar disorder depends on which zone the patient is in—either psychotic mania or psychotic depression.

For example, delusions in the depressed phase can be dreadful, and filled with self-hatred and paranoid ideas that the world is out to get them. They may believe that foreign governments or the CIA are spying on them, wanting to know their vast knowledge on world events. On the other hand, manic delusions are spectacular. But instead of just having great fantasies of stardom and glory, patients may actually believe they are living in those fantasies, as if they're really movie stars, great political leaders, or Internet millionaires.

These delusions in bipolar disorder are generally referred to as mood-congruent delusions because the content of the delusion tends to match the mood state. Typically, no psychotic symptoms are evident—that is, neither manic nor depressed—if the bipolar individual is in an in-between state. Schizophrenics, however, rarely have vast mood changes or an abatement of psychotic symptoms along with a mood change. That's what is noticed in bipolar disorder.

Identifying the causes of psychotic features, and whether or not they come and go in time, helps differentiate schizophrenia and bipolar disorder. Schizophrenia is regarded as a "thought disorder," which means a disorganized pattern of thoughts causes the psychosis and keeps it going. And because thoughts tend to be more consistent than feelings and evolve (or devolve) over time, the untreated psychotic features would be *pervasive*.

By comparison, in bipolar disorder, poorly regulated mood patterns—not thoughts—cause the psychosis. And because the moods change drastically, the psychosis comes and goes; it's *episodic*.

Typical treatments for bipolar disorder include certain antipsychotic medications also used for schizophrenia, so if a clinician cannot tell the difference between bipolar mania and schizophrenia right away, trying antipsychotics first may help. But it gets confusing when a patient thought to have schizophrenia suddenly gets better—not due to successful treatment but because the patient is bipolar and may have returned to the baseline mood zone. This complicates how treatment professionals think about the long-term care of that patient.

Substance Abuse

Substance abuse, which occurs frequently with bipolar disorder,[4] can make existing symptoms worse. Diagnosing bipolar separately from alcoholism and other drug abuse can be difficult. It's important to know which problem came first and which is driving the other. This is particularly true with severe stimulant abuse involving such drugs as methamphetamine and cocaine. These drugs can induce intense euphoria followed by grandiose feelings, pressured speech, and flight of ideas. Over time, these highly addictive substances can produce paranoia and psychotic symptoms. Alcoholism can increase irritability, hostility, and even thoughts and actions of violence. Abusing alcohol to quell agitation or lift depression also can lead to developing a dependency.

It's critical for a patient to achieve a measure of sobriety before fully assessing for bipolar disorder. Time away from alcohol and other drugs can provide an emotional "clean slate" to discover bipolar mood activity. But even before sobriety can be attempted, a personal history might reveal previous mood swings that occurred before substance abuse became a serious problem. (Look for further discussion on the effects of drugs on bipolar disorder in Chapter 5.)

Other Medical Disorders

Bipolar symptoms are mimicked by other disorders, so having a complete medical workup is a good idea. A history of thyroid imbalances could affect the diagnosis. In addition, postpartum hormonal imbalances in new mothers can induce a number of psychiatric problems, including bipolar. Traumatic brain injury, seizure disorders, and tumors can cause a bipolar-type presentation in those who have primary neurological disorders. Because bipolar symptoms typically emerge early in life, older people who show symptoms for the first time suggest an underlying medical cause for the psychiatric symptoms. This is especially true when there's a history of good mental health.

Patricia's Story

Patricia shares her struggle with reaching a bipolar diagnosis and how it inspires her to share her story with others:

> I've been an emotional wreck all my life. One second I'm calm, the next I am a bundle of nerves. At first I thought puberty was causing this emotional roller coaster, but as I got older, I realized it had to be something else. I spent years suffering before I searched for help. At first, my doctor treated me for anxiety, but after a few years he decided it was more than that. He referred me to a gynecologist thinking it was PMS (premenstrual syndrome). The gynecologist prescribed Prozac. After a while, she realized it was more than PMS, so she sent me to a psychiatrist. Finally, I was told I had bipolar disorder. We tried many

different medications, and eventually we found a combination of meds that worked.

I really want to help others who struggle with bipolar disorder and don't even know what's wrong with them.[5]

Different assessment methods are available to establish a good diagnosis. An additional opinion from another mental health professional can support or dispute a diagnosis of bipolar. Many patients and their families have gone through several professionals and multiple therapies or hospitalizations without success because a clear diagnosis wasn't made in the first place. With the proper knowledge of bipolar symptoms, and the ability to differentiate among other psychiatric problems, a precise assessment represents a good start in forming a viable treatment plan.

Notes

1. Pipich, M. (Writer/Director). (2013). Excerpts from friends from the bipolar network sharing their stories about living with bipolar [Radio series episode]. In M. Pipich (Producer), *Breakthrough with Michael Pipich*. Phoenix, AZ: VoiceAmerica Network.
2. Goldsmith M., Singh, M., & Chang, K. (2011). Antidepressants and psychostimulants in pediatric populations: Is there an association with mania? *Pediatric Drugs, 13*(4), 225–243.
3. Kernberg, O. (1985). *Borderline conditions and pathological narcissism*. New York: Jason Aronson, 29–34.
4. American Psychiatric Association. (2013). *Diagnostic and statistical manual of mental disorders* (5th ed.). Washington, DC: Author. 132–141.
5. Pipich, M. (Ed.) (2013). The bipolar network's shared stories. Retrieved December 1, 2013, from http://bipolarnetwork.com/shared-stories.html

CHAPTER 3

Why Bipolar Can Be Difficult to Accept

THE GOOD NEWS ABOUT TREATING bipolar disorder is there are several treatment options that can stabilize mood and help rebuild a functioning, healthy life. When it comes to treatment, what's the big deal?

Many people with bipolar simply don't seek out treatment, at least not willingly. And many more won't follow through with their treatment plans. In other cases, especially with bipolar adolescents, they might desire treatment but don't have the resources or support to maintain a treatment regime. Understanding the complexity of bipolar disorder is critical. More than that, successful treatment requires a full commitment from the patient *and* the patient's support system. That support system can include a spouse, family members, close friends, and work-related associates, along with treatment professionals. Without them actively assisting for the long term, treatment may be less effective or even abandoned.

Believe it or not, one of the biggest roadblocks to successful treatment of bipolar disorder is the belief that there is nothing to treat. What!?? Yes, you read that right. Many—both those who have bipolar, and those who love them—simply cannot accept that there is a problem.

Denial: A Common Defense Mechanism

The concept of denial, which is well-known among addiction specialists, has become part of common parlance and may be used in different contexts. We will now explore the common defense mechanism of denial in daily life and what it means for those with bipolar disorder.

Someone in denial is likely minimizing or refusing to accept some kind of painful reality. This isn't unusual in healthy people when they've been exposed to an extraordinary event. For example, if someone you know well died suddenly, you might say, "No, that can't be! I just talked to him yesterday!" In this case, denial is used to guard against an immediate and shocking kind of situation. We can all react this way in extraordinary circumstances. But when the shock wears off and reality sets in, we experience emotions of sadness, fear, maybe anger; but eventually we accept the reality to one extent or another, and move on with life. In this way, denial may actually help us cope with very difficult life events in the short term by keeping us safe from a complete psychological breakdown. As long as we don't hold on to it for very long, or allow it to interfere with other aspects of our daily lives, denial may give us a chance to orient ourselves in tough situations and process all the difficult emotions that follow.

But denial becomes a central psychological problem when it represents a consistent means by which an individual avoids facing personal responsibility, serious flaws in the self, and otherwise difficult changes necessary to accept a painful reality. In bipolar disorder, that painful reality often relates to the various consequences of depression and mania. The underlying fears of addressing those consequences, and ultimately facing the truth of how mania ruins life, keeps people with bipolar in denial.

For the purpose of this discussion, consider these three types of denial:

1. Simple denial
2. Minimization
3. Projection

Simple Denial. This is when someone simply denies the reality of an unpleasant fact. Example: "I don't know what you're talking about. I don't get manic."

Minimization. Here, the reality is admitted to an extent, but the denial has minimal significance. Example: "I guess you could say I get manic sometimes, but I don't hurt anyone."

Projection. Reality and significance are acknowledged to an extent, but blame is externalized, or "projected," onto others. Example: "Maybe I get manic, but if you were married to my wife, you'd be manic, too!"

"It's Not Mania. It's Creativity!"

What do Vincent van Gogh, Wolfgang Amadeus Mozart, Edgar Allan Poe, Ernest Hemingway, and Isaac Newton have in common? Besides brilliant minds that created classic works, they also are thought to have struggled with bipolar. So have entertainers Robin Williams, Jim Carrey, Richard Dreyfuss, Demi Lovato, Catherine Zeta-Jones, Ben Stiller,[1] and journalist Jane Pauley.[2] And let's not forget politicians Winston Churchill along with Theodore Roosevelt and Abraham Lincoln.[3] Add to that multiple entertainers, historical leaders, philosophers, inventors, entrepreneurs, journalists, authors, and mathematicians. Their zeal for creativity and productivity has enriched society beyond imagination.

Many with bipolar don't recognize their mania as a problematic state, especially when it gives them a sense of hypercreativity. When manic, people often feel very aroused in their thought process and energy level. As a result, they often believe they've discovered or extended their creative abilities beyond what they typically experience in baseline or depressive mood zones. Now, some people who are manic and hypercreative can certainly produce at a high rate. They typically experience this increased output at their jobs, recreational activities, and artistic endeavors. And they also usually feel quite special in their unique abilities when in that zone.

But for many others, their hypercreative state in bipolar becomes confused with their inflated self-esteem and grandiosity, and it may even reach delusional levels. The difference is in each individual's particular skill set. For instance, the great American author Ernest Hemingway most undoubtedly used his manic hypercreativity to write his classic novels; but there are those today who, while in that same condition, may really believe they're going to be the next Hemingway. If they don't have the abilities, experience, or credentials to be a great, adventurous, legendary author, they will rely only on those terrific feelings to affirm their "destiny." Exciting ideas will race through their expanded minds, and they will have no inhibitions telling others of their tremendous story lines. Someone in a delusional state may even quit a job or abandon a relationship in an undeniable pursuit of greatness. But without the skill, practice, and proper organization of writing a novel, that person's plans will evaporate when the mania goes away.

For those who do rely on hypercreativity in their skilled areas, they may find success in their chosen fields at some point. However, hypercreativity will not save them from poor health, broken relationships, or any of the other problems that accompany mania. Nor will it ever prevent them from becoming depressed or even suicidal, as in Hemingway's case.

It's often said there is a fine line between genius and madness. When we witness hypercreativity, we sometimes later see it free-fall into destruction—a self-annihilation to parallel the great-ness—and it leaves us wondering, "Why do these people who have it all want to throw it away?"

Truthfully, none of them *want* destruction, depression, or de-spair. It just may appear to go hand in hand with their exceptional abilities to produce at the highest levels. And even if they have moments of concern over their behavior, they quickly tap down these thoughts; they don't want to question this state of super well-being. If they recognize they have a problem, what would that mean to their careers? To their legacies? To the completion of their self-imposed duties to carry out their missions? As you progress through this book, you will see that true creativity doesn't come from bipolar itself, nor do people with bipolar "lose" creativity when they're in treatment. I'll show you how bipolar pa-tients can recover their unique skills and pursue organizational strategies to maintain consistent and successful creative ventures throughout a long and healthy life.

Mania Meets Perceived Needs

There are others with bipolar who recognize their mood swings, but accept—indeed, embrace—their mania as an antidote to their problems. How so? To understand what mania means to people with bipolar requires an ability to imagine a deep, desper-ate period of depression. It's a dark, bleak time when energy and motivation dissipate, and the body and mind feel empty, listless, or anxious. The colors of life darken into shades of gray, and all that felt warm and real in life deadens into a cold numbness.

To people with bipolar, mania is the only ticket out of that de-pression. Mania arouses the senses and stimulates the mind. Gray is replaced by Technicolor; the person begins to feel *alive* again. In a very real sense, mania is a relief. This is always true, even if the arousal process produces what most people find un-comfortable, such as irritability and agitation. People with bipolar often lack understanding of what "normal" is. Frequently, mania is perceived as the counterweight to depression. Once people have experienced a manic state, they can abandon the idea that baseline is the healthiest and safest place to be. They don't realize anymore that there is a place of balance between the poles of mania and depression. They just see mania as a desired alternative to the darkness.

They also know that depression will sideline them from productivity and life success. After having a taste of manic energy and hypercreativity, they soon recognize that depression has not only made them feel empty, numb, and lifeless, it has also up-ended all their amazing achievements. Becoming manic again is the only chance to "make up for lost time" after the nonproductivity and creative failure wrought by the depressive mood zone.

Thus, the bipolar perception is this: *As long as the manic phase can balance out the depressed phase, everything's fine.* People with bipolar employ a kind of irrational thinking as a defense against dealing with the reality of their true impairments. "Never mind what damage may be left in the aftermath of my manic episode," that irrational thinking goes. "Balance has been achieved, so there's no need to worry."

Denial and Fear of Mental Health Treatment

Denial can be a difficult matter to address. It helps to understand that denial in people with bipolar results from underlying fears.

I've found that, in general, people with bipolar fear treatment to a certain extent, regardless of age, gender, race, religion, cultural background, or educational level. Understandably people have concerns and fears about the treatment itself. They ask, "What does the treatment mean to who I am and how I'll live?"

Patients seek treatment (mainly psychotherapy) on their own or, for adolescents and young children, at the behest of their parents or school counselors. Unless they've already been diagnosed before seeing me in my practice, those I think have bipolar will present with all kinds of other mental health, substance abuse, or relationship problems. This is partly why bipolar conditions are easy to overlook.

Most patients who have an undetected bipolar disorder come to outpatient treatment for reasons other than mood swings—most commonly major depression and anxiety.[4] Life issues that emerge in therapy are usually relationship problems of any kind. In adults specifically, it's marriage problems. Substance abuse isn't easily admitted, and is marked by denial, but it's still commonly presented as a problem requiring serious attention.

When I've evaluated them and suggested bipolar disorder, several kinds of reactions follow. Some people are receptive to the concept and want to know more. Others greet the news with skepticism but still want to know what it means to them. A few reject the idea immediately. In all circumstances, though, fears emerge and, to some extent, denial.

As mentioned earlier, fears are a part of being human. The sophisticated way fears are constructed explains why the human species has been successful. That system of emotional memories and planning for trouble has kept us from being destroyed by the forces *around* us. But it's ironic that the same fear system so elegantly constructed to save our lives can hold us back from confronting the forces *within* us that put our lives—and perhaps the lives of those around us—at considerable risk.

Which brings us back to denial.

Understanding the defense of denial requires being familiar with the concept of "fight or flight." This is the brain's natural response when it perceives danger (either actually happening or expected to happen). When adrenaline reaches the brain, we prepare to *fight*—either to attack the other or defend ourselves. The *flight* response is to run away from the threat.

Discussing denial in bipolar disorder doesn't refer to a *physical* fight or flight; it's a *mental* type of fight or flight. A mental *fight* would be actively guarding an emotionally painful truth to keep it from entering rational thought. This can take the form of disagreeing or using elaborate methods to repel that truth.

A mental *flight* is harder to identify than a mental *fight*, but it can take various forms of "checking out"—including substance abuse or reckless behavior. Running *away* from a painful truth almost always leads to running *toward* destructive activity. This is why people in denial can create complex entanglements in their social and occupational lives. And they get especially complicated in the lives of people with bipolar.

I've stated that denial in people with bipolar results from underlying fears, but what specific fears are those? Here are typical ones:

- Losing the energy and creativity experienced when manic
- Being depressed all the time without the offset of mania
- Having to face consequences from manic episodes
- Losing personal identity (a sense of who they are)
- Becoming boring and dull
- Having to take medications every day
- Having to reduce or give up alcohol or recreational drugs
- Feeling "like a zombie" on medications
- Being the "sick one" in the family
- Being the "crazy one" in a relationship
- Getting "locked up" in a psychiatric facility
- Being forever stigmatized as mentally ill

Family members dealing with bipolar disorder also have fears—primarily that their bipolar loved ones won't get into treatment or stick with it. But they can live in denial, too. Spouses, siblings, adult children, and parents can be afraid of the bipolar diagnosis and what needs to be done about it. While most family members eventually suffer the consequences of bipolar mood swings, they can sometimes feel periods of relief when their bipolar loved ones are coming out of an extreme mood zone toward baseline. Temporary periods of calm and rational behavior in a bipolar patient can cause a family member to think, *Okay every-*

thing's fine now. Or they may try to tolerate some level of mania or hypomania, believing that their passionate, energetic loved one has come "back to life" after a period of dark depression. Overall, they may fear that discussing the problem of bipolar will actually provoke the very worst aspects of the illness. This dynamic can delay or complicate getting the right treatment for the patient and the family members.

Tom's Story

Tom passionately detailed how the denial in those around him affected his own denial, as he said:

> I really wish people would stop telling me that there is nothing wrong with me…that my condition doesn't exist. How do they know what's going on with me? Look, I wish I wasn't bipolar. It's not easy.
>
> You know, if everyone keeps saying I don't have bipolar, well…maybe I'll believe them. Maybe everything I've been holding myself back from doing during an episode is just fine to do. Maybe I don't have to work so hard, and maybe this whole treatment thing is a waste of time. If they act like I'm not bipolar, why should I protect them from it?

Breaking Through Denial

Addressing denial in the bipolar patient is part of the first step of treatment. No one wants to fear that whatever makes them feel good is exposed as something bad and possibly taken away. Bipolar patients feel that way about their mania just as addicts feel about their drug of choice (remember, mania is a defense against depression). Moreover, a manic episode often is marked by grandiose self-image, hypercreativity, and productivity. The need to defend these as positive attributes of bipolar disorder makes it difficult to repackage them as personal flaws, or worse, symptoms of a chronic disease.

Knowing that denial in bipolar disorder is a defense against specific fears, and that mania is a perceived balance against severe depression, allows us to confront denial in the life of a person with bipolar. We aren't confronting the *person*; we know people with bipolar have an affliction that isn't their fault. We're confronting a defense that guards against the fears inherent with this affliction.

The approach begins with identifying and understanding those fears, and then addressing them in an emotionally safe environment, such as the therapist's office. By working through them, a person with bipolar can take ownership of the disorder while maintaining a sense of his or her dignity.

How do therapists confront the person with bipolar who's in denial? They could start by asking, "What is it about admitting you have bipolar disorder and getting treatment that's so scary for you?"

Believe it or not, some people answer that question directly, making life easier for everyone. But that doesn't happen often. Inquiries should be direct but delivered with more technique and finesse. Precise attention to the person's word choice, emotional demeanor (known as "affect"), and overall content of the responses to this subject can provide insights about the patient's fears.

Everyone is different and requires different approaches. I get to know patients and family members so I can determine the best way to speak to them. The following examples represent some typical reactions from patients and what I've said in return. That way, you can better understand how to confront denial in your own circumstances.

> PATIENT 1: I only get depressed at times. When I'm not
> depressed, things are really good.

[This tells me the patient doesn't see mania as bad, only depression. Mania still is perceived as a defense against depression. I may just focus on depression prevention as an opening to discuss mania's role in the overall disease.]

ME: Your history tells me your brain's response to depression can go to extremes. It probably does feel good to get as far away from depression as possible, and it's scary to think you could go back to depression. Let's talk about better ways to keep you away from depression, without the fear of returning to that dark place.

PATIENT 2: I came here for marriage counseling, and now you're telling me I'm the problem?

ME: I believe you and your husband both have issues that contribute to your marriage problems. They're not all because of you. But the bipolar disorder has to be treated first. Otherwise, we won't get to do what you hope to accomplish. All we have to do is start the bipolar treatment. Then I can really help you address the concerns you're having with your husband.

PATIENT 3: If my boss finds out about this, I'm toast.

[Explaining the rules of confidentiality in therapy is not always enough. With so much of their lives at stake, I don't expect everyone to trust therapy right away. Patients can also fear losing control of the process.]

ME: Our treatment is totally confidential, but I can understand your fears about not having control over this. My concern is if you go untreated, people may find out about your bipolar through your behavior, and then you won't have control over what happens to your job or your life.

PATIENT 4: I don't like taking pills.

[This is a common, generic statement that can reflect any number of concerns over medications. Sometimes it has nothing to do with meds, though. It could be just an easy way to deflect the topic. Nonetheless, I find it handy to continue the conversation.]

> ME: I understand. Nobody likes taking pills. But everyone has different reasons for that. I'd like to know your reasons.

Family members can be in denial, too. Here are typical comments from loved ones and how I might handle them:

> SPOUSE: I don't believe in bipolar disorder. It's just an excuse for my husband's bad behavior.

[Spouses often feel hurt by the consequences of the disorder. Even when treatment starts, they still worry their own pain won't be addressed.]

> ME: Bipolar disorder is never an excuse for bad behavior. It's an explanation of what's been going on. With that explanation, your husband can begin taking ownership of that behavior, and we can talk honestly about how it's affected you.

> PARENT: Doctors love to label kids. My son doesn't need to be branded for life.

[At this moment, the parent isn't worried about all "doctors," as much as he or she is afraid of what I'm going to do to the child. But all parents worry about their children having a lifelong illness. Parents prefer to think their child can outgrow anything, so I start with more immediate concerns that most parents share.]

ME: I agree that your son needs to be treated with great care. I'm not out to label him but to help him do his best. I do know that kids with bipolar can have all sorts of serious problems in school, at home, and in society. For example, they're more likely to abuse drugs or alcohol. And those problems could continue for a long time if not treated properly. So, let's talk more about how bipolar treatment can help with the goals you have for your son in the short term.

In any of these examples, the most important objective is to keep the discussion alive and focus it on the fears underlining the denial. Although we maintain a sense of urgency, not all matters involving bipolar disorder are meant to be accomplished fast. Confronting denial is about identifying and addressing fears. Working through those fears builds trust and, ultimately, collaboration toward owning bipolar.

In all human relationships, we must seek understanding over agreement. That's when agreement can develop organically and have greater strength for the long haul.

Your Own Denial

As you read this, you might be thinking about your own denial. Good! Go deeper about your true fears as you acknowledge having a bipolar problem. Seek help for it, then reach out to others—personal and professional—for feedback on your behavior. From there, you can more clearly match those fears and your reactions accurately.

If you're thinking about a bipolar loved one who is in denial, good for you! Denial can be frustrating to break through, and feeling like giving up is understandable. Although you can't make others do what they should, your interactions with that person with bipolar can take on an understanding and supportive tone. When their manic behavior is brash and energetic, it's hard to imagine they're actually fearful human beings. But by acknowledging they have fears and knowing what they might be, you improve your chances of getting loved ones to accept their bipolar situation and seek treatment.

Notes

1. Ruth, S. L. (2014, August 14). Update: Celebrities, like Robin Williams, with depression and bipolar disorder. *Communities Digital News*. Retrieved September 19, 2016, from http://www.commdiginews.com/health-science/health/five-celebrities-besides-robin-williams-with-bipolar-disorder-23601/
2. CBS News (n.d.). Famous people with bipolar disorder. Retrieved May 5, 2016, from http://www.cbsnews.com/pictures/famous-people-celebrities-bipolar
3. Fieve, R. R. (1997). *Moodswing*. (2nd ed.). New York: Bantam Books. 127–153.
4. McIntyre, R. S. (2014). Improving the early recognition and diagnosis of bipolar disorder. *Journal of Clinical Psychiatry*, 75(2), e03.

CHAPTER 4

• • • • • •

Understanding the Bipolar Experience

ALTHOUGH IT'S IMPORTANT TO UNDERSTAND what bipolar looks like—such as identifiable symptoms and the defense of denial around those symptoms—it's also good to know how people who live those symptoms feel. This is necessary for family members, so they can better relate to the complex and often painful struggles that accompany the disorder. Too often, family members insist that their bipolar loved ones should simply understand how bad the mood swings can be, but don't understand themselves why it may be so hard to give up mania and get to treatment right away. Likewise, people with bipolar disorder sometimes believe that no one can possibly understand what they experience, causing a sense of separation from their families and the world around them. Understanding the bipolar experience can help to bridge gaps between patients and families for improved communication and empathy for everyone who lives with the disorder.

The purpose of this chapter is to provide some ideas and examples of what manic and depressive experiences are like for people

53

with bipolar disorder. No two personal bipolar experiences are exactly alike. But when reading this chapter, know the information comes from statements and experiences from many different individuals with bipolar disorder, and drawn together to form some common shared experiences. If you are a person who may have bipolar disorder, some ideas may sound familiar, some may not. But I recommend you use this as a guide to look a bit deeper into your own bipolar experience so that you can communicate your feelings and ideas to those who may need to better understand what you're going through. If you're a family member, you can use these concepts to create a greater understanding into why bipolar can be so difficult to give up. Then, you can better confront bipolar disorder, instead of just confronting the person with bipolar.

The Manic Experience

In defining bipolar disorder in general and mania in particular, mental health professionals search for specific symptoms that provide *objective* information for diagnosis and treatment. That means collecting data through observation and history, and then matching that data with a list of bipolar criteria gathered and researched scientifically among many large study groups. That's how we've derived the symptoms necessary to diagnose bipolar mood swings, which were discussed earlier.

Subjective refers to an individual patient's inner experience of mania. Although many qualities may be common to other people with bipolar, subjective experiences represent the unique story of this person's illness. People who have been manic in its different forms report different experiences that help account for their often troubling behaviors. So, the objective information obtained in an evaluation and personal history helps establish diagnosis and early treatment needs. But it's the subjective information that gives us the true identity of that one individual's bipolar story, and what problems and issues may come up in therapy.

The following are some examples of what it's like to be manic from the subjective experiences of others.

Events and experiences during a manic episode can be so accelerated that the person loses track of time and a clear sense of purpose. The adage "time flies when you're having fun" has a greater meaning in mania. The urge to soar through the episode and achieve as much as possible is overwhelming. Although some activities may be considered productive, many others are not. And often, typical adult responsibilities of work, finances, and/or relationships are neglected or harmed. Through the experience, denial is an active component in the bluster of activity pushed by mania. This often presents as either simple denial or minimization, both of which are used to avoid a serious review of manic consequences. During this episode a person may not pay bills, binge drink through a bar-hopping spree, or miss important dates and appointments without any notice.

But, when the episode ends, patients often report failing to recall things they did or said. Those around them might call this amnesia "convenient" or "selective," but generally their usual memory process is fractured during the manic episode. Once they enter a different mood zone, they often don't remember everything that happened.

Over time, they might figure out what they did and said by recovering certain memories, but more likely they find out from other sources. Family or friends tell them what happened during mania, but they might meet a full account with skepticism. Or they might discover the extent of their behaviors after getting arrested or winding up in a hospital—results that are difficult to dispute or reject. Unexpected credit card charges or other strange bills can come due, delivering a shocking chronology of manic exploits. Drug or alcohol binges—especially when ending in a mammoth hangover—can provide proof of an underlying manic process that could destroy any hope of maintaining a life of sobriety.

In a return to the baseline zone, they may come to believe—at least to some extent—that something is wrong with them. But commonly, the failure to remember certain events, even in the face of undeniable evidence, can still lead to excuses and denial. With their sense of shame too heavy to bear, they can turn to the form of denial known as projection—blaming others for their apparent failures. For example, if bills are overdue, the person with bipolar may say to a spouse, "Don't blame me for those bills. You should've paid them. I was too busy!"

If you've never been manic, it's hard to relate to how the increased feelings of energy, creativity, and grandiosity can drive you to do things beyond all reason. One way to imagine this is to recall the best dream you've ever had. Maybe you once dreamed you were a powerful king of your own country and commanded your own army. Maybe you dreamed you were a virtuoso concert pianist with your fingers flying along the keyboard and the audience on its feet (though you've never played anything more than "Chopsticks" in real life). Or maybe you dreamed that as bullies chased you, you managed to climb a wall, jump up, and fly over the rooftops of your neighborhood, feeling light and wonderful.

People in a manic state are, literally, living a dream. The more severe the mania, especially when in a psychotic mood zone, the more that behavior reflects a mind acting out its greatest fantasies. These fantasies can reveal desires of great wealth, power, ambition, popularity, and sexual conquest. In truth, these are wishes buried deep within the unconscious that all humans possess. The unconscious part of the mind holds our desires and fears, but they're frequently kept away from our immediate awareness. Although we entertain fantasies within the privacy of our conscious mind or even in measured actions, we tend to keep the most destructive desires and fears under control. But in the throes of mania, the intense energy and grandiosity pushes out the conscious ability to maintain that control.

Bipolar disorder patients in treatment have described experiencing their manic episodes as if watching a movie of someone else instead of living it themselves. They describe a sense of surrealism; it feels intense and super-real in the moment but at the same time not exactly real. Doesn't that sound like how we experience dreams? They seem real until we wake up, and even then it takes a while before we recognize our conscious state and realize everything that just happened actually didn't. Commonly, we forget large swaths of the dreams we just experienced.

It's logical to see much of the subjective manic experience coming from deep, unconscious desires. These desires are raw, unprocessed, and unfiltered mental material similar to nightly dreams. Recall the discussion of the amygdala, the deeply embedded part of the brain that processes old emotional memories. It's not difficult to imagine our deepest unconscious feelings come from within our brains, and that they're generating material for our dreams. Although this material can manifest as disjointed and chaotic, it originates from within.

Similarly, the amygdala could be actively generating material for a manic episode. That material is unfiltered by brain structures such as the prefrontal cortex (PFC) that support reason and good judgment. We rely on having a properly functioning brain to manage our emotions, desires, and fears through homeostasis (balance). The periodic loss of this functioning due to bipolar disorder renders a person incapable of acting with a freedom of choice. It's this factor—freedom of choice—that defines our true identity apart from our deepest desires and fears.

Consider a man who, when in a baseline mood zone, strives to be a good, faithful husband. But when he's manic, he trolls the bars searching for indiscriminate sexual encounters. Which behavior really defines him? Is he Dr. Jekyll or Mr. Hyde? Or is he actually both at the same time—a kind of split personality?

People with bipolar and their loved ones struggle with this question all the time. When it comes to bipolar disorder, who "the real person is" can be best determined when the brain is treated with medications to improve its homeostasis. Medications don't define the real person. Rather, he or she can be discovered when medications effectively stabilize mood swings.

How does this relate to the wandering husband? If his conscious efforts to be faithful dominate his baseline periods, it's predictable that stabilizing medications will assist him in maintaining his goal of marital fidelity.

Yet, some may argue that he still has a deeply embedded desire to cheat on his wife. Medications will not resolve the underlying and unconscious motivators—and he knows it. Those deeper conflicts may continue to frustrate him, especially because he has already acted on them. He recognizes that bipolar disorder is an explanation, not an excuse. But that's not good enough. He wants to understand why his mania pushed him in that direction when other people with bipolar never cheat on their spouses. Thus, after a period of being stable, it's necessary to examine those deep desires to resolve his relevant subjective issues.

Perhaps answering questions about his upbringing reveals he had a particularly difficult sexual coming-of-age. Maybe his adolescence and young adulthood were fraught with rejection, guilt, and confusion. Even if his marriage is satisfying, bipolar mania gave him a sense of sexual prowess he'd always dreamed of having. After getting stabilized, he would have the opportunity to grieve and resolve the emotional pain of his interpersonal and sexual development beyond bipolar disorder. That would allow him to live more truthfully in his marriage.

Maria's Story

Maria, when manic, leaves home for long stretches of time. She checks in to hotels, striking up bizarre conversations with hotel guests and staff and running up large tabs. She sometimes travels far from home, and after the manic episode doesn't know how she wound up in a different city.

Taking stabilizing medications quells her impulse to run away, but why did she act that way in the first place? In a psychotherapy session after she was stabilized, she recalled how her father abandoned the family when she was young. She remembered he was a salesman who would leave town for long periods, but his return was always assured. However, one day he left and never came back. His absence was never discussed or explained to her. She had always longed for his return, wondering where he went. And because she needed his love and attention, she experienced a misplaced sense of guilt for not being "good enough" for her father to stay with her.

In therapy, Maria came to understand that she repressed her true feelings, especially because as a child, she was not permitted to speak openly about the abandonment. Instead, the mania gave her a "voice" to express herself. She had a sense of power she never felt as a helpless, reticent child. Eventually, she also learned that feelings of guilt are common in abandonment, and they could be transformed into healthy expressions of anger. She came to understand that the deeper desires emerging in the manic episode related to searching and finding her father—both to hug him and punch him in the face for leaving. This greater awareness gave her the opportunity to heal at a deeper level beyond medications alone.

Keep in mind that traumatic experiences alone don't cause bipolar disorder; a person must have a predisposition for bipolar. However, unresolved conflicts—big and small—are part of life, and those conflicts dwelling within each of us gain momentum if we don't consciously attend to them. The less we seek to understand our unconscious conflicts, the more power they have. In the way these conflicts play out in our nightly dreams, they can also power the subjective manic experience.

But just because mania can make an everyday Joe feel like Napoleon, Casanova, or Magellan doesn't mean all people with bipolar are meek simpletons when they're in the baseline zone. They're not Clark Kent waiting for mania to convert them into Superman. Some are intellectual giants, eccentric innovators, or charismatic leaders who can live their passions without the drive of mania.

Even in their own baseline mood zone, these individuals can often live in the fast lane in ways that are incomprehensible to most outsiders. They may routinely engage in risky recreational pursuits, multiple sexual encounters, or impulsive business decisions as an actual part of their baseline experience. While they may appear manic all the time to others, they are more supercharged people, who at certain points, are quite functional, in spite of their flirtation with impulsivity and peril. They can be hyperproductive in enviable ways, but at some point that fast lane ends at a wall. That wall is a true shift in mood to their own manic mood zone. And when they do enter the manic zone, they ultimately "crash and burn" as a result of that mania.

But despite the inevitability of the crash, they keep going. If they have achieved or are achieving something that's amazing, they pursue greatness at all costs. They're hell-bent on continuing because deep within their unconscious, they know they're not immortal or they may have already convinced themselves that their lives will be shortened by their behavior anyway, so they attempt to achieve as much glory and pleasure as possible. The conflict fueling their mania can be a ticking clock—one that could easily transform into a ticking time bomb during the manic mood zone. This is often when mania becomes the most life-threatening time of their lives.

In all subjective manic experiences, bipolar disorder is entirely a disorder of mood, not of thought. It might appear that a manic person's thoughts are disordered, but instead, the disordered mood state is essentially crowding out any semblance of rational thought. Patients sometimes describe the "feeling-action" response to an impulse that's influenced by the mood episode, and followed by immediate action. The action is not preceded by any rational thought to evaluate whether or not it's the right action to take socially, morally, or by any reasonable standard. This is another good example of what I mentioned earlier about bipolar brain functions. The PFC, which is responsible for rational evaluation of behavior, does not slow the reactivity of the amygdala during mania. Instead, there is a sense of greatness and pleasure that goes with the feeling before the action. It's not that the ability to think rationally is forever gone—it's just been pushed out by the manic process.

Mania is often a series of these responses: Feeling, action. Feeling, action. Feeling, action. Feeling, action. And the person justifies each action because the feeling dictates the action without any competing thought to evaluate it. So, when in the manic zone, people feel *right* about their actions because of the temporary loss of understanding that what they did was actually *wrong*. You might hear a person who has been through mania describe their feeling-action behaviors this way: "Because I didn't think what I was doing was wrong, I felt it was right." This sequence keeps going without intermittent review, other than the overarching euphoric or dysphoric manic feelings that feed and maintain the repeating pattern.

Cindy's Story

During bipolar therapy, a young patient named Cindy recognized that her ability to think clearly during her manic mood zone was closed off, especially when it might evaluate a certain *feeling* against a potential *action*. When manic, she didn't think her responses were wrong because she couldn't assess what could possibly be wrong about her behavior. Based entirely on her feelings, she felt her actions were always right!

Once during a manic episode, she was so angry at her father, her feeling resulted in grabbing a flower vase and throwing it at him. She had no immediate sense of what she was doing or that she should have done anything different.

After taking antimanic medication for a few days, Cindy, said, "A little space opened up between the feeling and the action. It was just enough to have a thought about what I was going to do." And it was enough for her to accept that something had been wrong all along. After that "little space" of thinking reopened through medication, she was better able to assess her potential action, instead of acting out in the feeling of anger. She could still have that feeling, but her PFC could slow down the impulsive activity coming from the amygdala. No longer was she governed by the feeling-action response.

The Depressive Experience

It's difficult for anyone who has never experienced major depression to relate to the overwhelming sense of hopelessness, loss of motivation, and feelings of desperation. You know what it's like to feel down, frustrated with life, or deeply saddened over a loss. But major ongoing depression can be psychologically—sometimes physically—debilitating. Some cases last for several consecutive days, others much longer. Depression possesses an all-consuming quality that sets it apart from any other mood state. And when it hits people with bipolar, it hits them especially hard.

To imagine the depressive experience, recall the worst dream you ever had. Maybe you had nightmares of getting physically stuck or paralyzed amid loud noises or frightening visions. Maybe marauding monsters—animal, alien, or subhuman—cornered you, assaulted you, or incapacitated you in some manner. Instead of flying with the greatest of ease, you're in free-fall as you close in on the inevitable crash. Or perhaps your worst dream involves needing to get somewhere important, but you're constantly losing things you need to get there. Nobody helps you; nobody cares. You feel isolated and alone.

Beyond the objective symptoms, this is how depression can be *subjectively* experienced in real life. The worse the depression, especially at the psychotic level, the more the sense of isolation is experienced as a permanent reality. In fact, life no longer seems like a painful struggle but instead a losing battle. Everyone else is winning the battle at the depressed person's expense. Profound feelings of hopelessness and helplessness make it difficult to even get out of bed . . . because, why bother?

Remember how stuck you felt in your dream? You wanted desperately to move, but something held you back. And despite your cries, nobody would help. If you can imagine how supreme desires in mania can create the acting out of dreamlike material, you can do the same for the depressive experience. But at this level, it's not about feelings of grandeur. It's about every terrifying fear buried deep within the mind.

Major depression often is the first mood event for people with bipolar disorder. In fact, they can have several depressive events before mania or hypomania kicks in. People with bipolar often hold a strong sense of low self-esteem, and can feel anxiety about failure and loneliness through various mood zones. But when depressed, people with bipolar can experience severe emotional pain. They might even suffer a paralyzing numbness that feels like death.

Appreciating the subjective depressive experiences of people with bipolar helps you understand their need to protect their mania. If you can relate to what it's like to be psychologically and physically stuck in an awful place, it's easier to appreciate why mania is so alluring. For some, there's a sense of relief that they've escaped the clutches of depression, like feeling released from their own personal prison. Others may even view post-depression mania as their personal salvation—like a deep, spiritual experience.

However, the manic episode doesn't always lift the person with bipolar out of stagnation and into productivity and grand achievement. Sometimes the underlying conflicts in the depressive experience are the flip side of the manic experience.

Gloria's Story

Gloria, a student with bipolar, remarked that she constantly struggled with school despite her intelligence. This struggle produced profound feelings of failure. She felt terribly "different" from her peers and believed she could never succeed in any aspect of life.

Those underlying issues were common to all of her mood zones. But how did they present themselves in bipolar overall? Her answer: "Manic tells me, 'Don't do your schoolwork; you don't need to because you're better than that.' Depression says, 'What does it matter? It's not like you'll get into college.'"[1] The difference occurs in how she avoids her struggle with academics based on which mood zone she's in.

I believe Gloria feels depressed most of the time. Each mania episode becomes a respite from her constant fear and self-loathing. Therefore, her treatment needs to extend beyond mood stabilization. She has to also deal with her self-image struggles over meeting her academic and social potential.

Long-term bipolar treatment approaches are more weighted toward avoiding *depression* than avoiding *mania*. After all, avoiding depression may be what people with bipolar are essentially attempting to do—if not consciously, then through the brain's unconscious systems. When bipolar patients begin to experience how depression can be prevented, without the offset of manic episodes, they begin to trust the treatment process and discover how to use it for further life gains.

Ron's Story

Ron returns to therapy on occasion even though his bipolar has been well-managed for a long time. He's a good example of *owning bipolar* because he recognizes every new life challenge holds the possibility for depression. Dealing with challenges in his job, marriage, parenting, and other areas of his life motivates him to set an appointment. He can work through the effects of changes that, if unchecked, would throw him into a depressive mood zone.

When Ron comes into my office, he rarely mentions anything about mania although he has lived its consequences. What's far clearer to him, however, is how depressive episodes caused him to hate his life and contemplate ending it. Just as his medication is oriented toward preventing bipolar depression, his therapy is set to keep his mood relatively elevated.

After a few sessions to discuss the current challenges in his life and how best to resolve them, he experiences a confident return to baseline. Any recurrence of mood swings—first from depression, then toward mania—has been averted.

Notes

1. McIntyre, R. S. (2014). Improving the early recognition and diagnosis of bipolar disorder. *Journal of Clinical Psychiatry, 75*(2), e03.

CHAPTER 5

Bipolar Therapy: A Three-Phase Approach

ALTHOUGH BIPOLAR DISORDER HAS EXISTED throughout recorded history, only recently have various psychological remedies been tested. Therapies based in psychological examination and discussion were often tried, but it appeared that many of the treatments didn't succeed. But then something interesting happened. Once the mood stabilizer lithium was introduced to treat mood swings, many therapists were taught that medication was the *only* treatment necessary for bipolar disorder. The concept was simple. Bipolar disorder was deemed resistant to traditional talk-based therapies, so it was essential to get patients on medication—especially lithium—and ensure they stay on it. Many came to believe the one-hour therapy session could be replaced by a brief med check. And this concept was handed down to succeeding generations of therapists who primarily followed that approach to treating bipolar disorder.

Early in my training, I was provided the same concept, as were many of my peers. "Just get them on meds and keep them there" was the prevailing mind-set. However, some therapists recognized the needs of bipolar patients extended beyond just taking medication, so not all agreed with the "meds-only" concept (including myself). But because previous talk-based therapies didn't stabilize mood swings in the way lithium could, meds-only became embedded into the overall approach to bipolar disorder on a large scale. I believe this meds-only idea has reduced the profession's ability to treat bipolar in a comprehensive and consistent manner. It doesn't lend itself to a collaborative approach, it doesn't address mania as a defense against depression, and it doesn't understand the long-term needs of patients and families after medication is prescribed.

Today we need a therapy approach that addresses the needs of patients and families facing a bipolar-disorder diagnosis. This approach highlights medications as essential in treatment, but never is limited to them. It also recognizes how family support is an important part of the overall treatment, from early crisis through lifelong care. And I believe knowing this three-phase approach can help you understand and address all therapy needs and concerns as you go through treatment with your professional team.

In my work with bipolar patients, I approach therapy in three phases:

1. Pre-stabilization phase
2. Stabilization phase
3. Post-stabilization phase

The word "stabilization" refers specifically to achieving mood levels that are clinically acceptable. But for our purposes, it marks an overall part of bipolar treatment, and the standard by which we judge the phases before and after. Next, I will define each phase.

Pre-stabilization

The pre-stabilization phase of bipolar therapy is marked by:

- Crisis
- Assessment for bipolar disorder
- Denial
- Treating the symptoms

Crisis

The first phase of care is marked mostly by a crisis that is caused or affected by bipolar. This phase could have been going on for a long time in the life of a person with bipolar, perhaps since childhood. Recall that there's an average span of ten years between the first bipolar mood event and proper bipolar treatment. For the treating clinician, however, this phase is first recognized when bipolar is diagnosed, even if the patient didn't come in for bipolar disorder in the first place.

People with bipolar often seek treatment for other reasons. They find themselves in crisis and want help based on their understanding of that crisis. Marital problems, anxiety, work-related issues, and substance abuse are common complaints. Depression often is a reason, too, although without the complaints associated with mania.

But at times, a patient who has no intention of seeking treatment gets a referral from emergency room physicians when a manic crisis or suicide attempt occurs. Attorneys or probation officers also refer individuals whose bipolar crisis resulted in legal troubles. A school counselor or human resource manager might intervene when an apparent mood episode affects performance or disturbs classmates and coworkers. And in severe circumstances, the pre-stabilization crisis could result in an inpatient hospital admission.

Assessment

No matter how or why the patient comes to treatment, similar conditions and approaches apply to each situation. The therapist might specifically evaluate for mood disorders (including bipolar disorder) before starting treatment for other psychological ailments, or before noticing symptoms that point to bipolar. In either case, the therapist has work to do to introduce patients to the idea that their problems result from bipolar disorder.

Bipolar symptoms are first noticeable in pre-stabilization, and they are often seen by themselves as separate problems, or not as problems at all. Disagreement among the patient, therapist, and family members can occur as a result. A patient or family member may question if a single bipolar symptom is a problem. As a therapist, I point out as many bipolar symptoms as I can uncover, not only to make a correct diagnosis but also to explain these symptoms one by one to the patient. For example, a bipolar patient may view high increases of energy as a good thing because of a surge in productivity. But a spouse may associate that energy with wildly impulsive behavior that leads to excessive spending. Even so, that same spouse may not see that symptom by itself as connected to a broader clinical disorder known as bipolar. It may just be thought of as bad morals.

The more I can present a list of symptoms to patients, the more difficult it is for them to argue against the symptoms' importance, even if a few of those symptoms are not individually viewed as problems. I may not emphasize the increased energy as a significant problem, but instead link it to other evident symptoms, like impulsivity, distractibility, and racing thoughts. And I may say to both the patient and spouse, "I know the increased energy feels great, but it comes along with other symptoms that interfere with your ability to think and act clearly. These symptoms add up to a greater problem." Then I explain how impulsive actions, distractibility, and racing thoughts comprise the larger problem of bipolar, and don't reflect the moral character of the person. Likewise, I'll add how that rush of energy leads to the eventual onset of depression and cite those particular symptoms, as well.

Denial

Denial—often a roadblock to owning bipolar—is a main feature of pre-stabilization. Therapists expect a level of denial in this phase and don't view their patients as merely being uncooperative. Because bipolar patients come to therapy for a variety of reasons, they don't like to be told their problems originate from something *inside them,* especially if they're having relationship issues. To address denial requires the therapist to discuss bipolar disorder on the basis of symptoms. Rather than going back and forth with the patient or family about bipolar itself, a productive discussion starts by breaking down the disorder into understandable—and hard to argue—components.

Treating the Symptoms

The patient doesn't consider all symptoms "terrible." Euphoria, creative ideas, and boundless energy are difficult to address as "problems." Symptoms such as irritability and restlessness are regarded as more problematic than manic symptoms. And depression is never good. Because bipolar is defined more by mania and hypomania than depression alone, the focus falls on high-end mood zones, but depression must always be a part of the discussion.

That's why I usually start with symptoms that are viewed as problematic. These include:

- Depressed mood (depression)
- Irritability and restlessness (depression/mania)
- Anxiety (depression/mania)
- Loss of energy and interest in usual activities (depression)
- Changes in sleep (depression/mania)
- Guilt and worthlessness (depression)
- Loss of concentration (depression/mania)
- Avoidance of life responsibilities (depression/mania)

- Social or occupational impairments (depression/mania)
- Acts of self-harm (depression/mania)
- Suicidal thoughts or actions (depression/mania)

For example, when a patient says, "When I'm feeling up, I can get so much work done," we also talk about how little gets accomplished with the eventual loss of concentration and changes in sleep. Or a patient who has acknowledged bouts of both mania and severe depression could argue, "I can feel so good about myself, why should I give that up?" The reply might be, "Yes, and I'm sure you're worried about losing that great feeling. But I'm concerned about how you also crash into thoughts of suicide. I'd like to talk about how that doesn't have to be a problem in your life."

Without forcing the negative issues, the conversational approach separates and highlights the "bad" aspects from the perceived "good" to provide a comprehensive discussion on all bipolar symptoms.

Primarily, pre-stabilization refers to the phase of bipolar assessment that addresses denial surrounding the diagnosis and how it affects life and relationships. It's when a medication conversation with patients and families occurs (discussed in Chapter 6). This phase usually isn't clean and neat. Patients often struggle with relinquishing the perceived control of their lives to treatment. In this phase, agreeing to treatment usually implies a provisional consent to proceed, but without fully accepting bipolar as a lifelong disorder.

If you're a new bipolar patient or a loved one grappling with early treatment, know that therapy needs to be oriented around immediate bipolar symptoms, including a few that don't seem like much of a problem by themselves. Soon enough, therapy can move toward treating the full disorder. In pre-stabilization, you're likely confronting a crisis started or worsened by bipolar symptoms, no matter what other problems you may be facing. You may feel frustrated that your original issues, like relationship or legal problems, are set aside to focus on bipolar symptoms. If your other concerns seem forgotten, never fear. The best outcomes in therapy, and in life, are done once the symptoms are fully addressed and mood swings are abated.

As a patient or family member, feel free to inquire both about how specific bipolar therapy proceeds and when you can expect a return to the therapy issues that concern you the most. It's good practice to remind your professional team you're interested in the complete therapy package. Assure your team you're prepared to do what it takes to meet the treatment objectives.

Stabilization

The stabilization phase is marked by:

- Finding the right medications
- Accepting bipolar as a lifelong mental illness
- Treating the entire disorder

The challenges in this phase typically make early treatment uneven. It's common for patients to forget appointments, neglect to take meds regularly, or just lack the energy and enthusiasm to stay focused on the immediate goals. The stabilization phase is notably a rough go for any number of reasons. These can include sacrifices of time and money for appointments, the continuing effects of unstabilized mood swings, an incomplete acceptance of the need for treatment, or simply an absence of hope. It's important to acknowledge the inherent struggles of this phase so patients and families understand that, although difficult, many people have come through it successfully.

Bipolar symptom treatment includes introducing medication specific to bipolar disorder. (These medications and their effects will be presented in Chapter 7.) While finding the right medications is the centerpiece of bipolar treatment, various challenges go into the stabilization process. For example, it can take a while for the patient to make the doctor's appointment, get and fill a prescription, and start taking the medications. The first round of medications can take anywhere from a few days to a few weeks to take effect, depending on the type of medication and its characteristics. Even then, the doctor might have to adjust the medication. That's because doctors sometimes want to start with lower doses and work up to higher ones, or discover during a med trial that another drug may be better suited for that patient.

Simply taking meds isn't enough for stabilization to occur. In modern-day psychiatry, room for trial and error must exist. Doctors can make good judgments on which medication to start with. However, every patient has unique physical and mental qualities, and medication adjustments typically are needed until the right combination and dosages are met for that individual. Along with the right meds, a good dose of patience and confidence is needed during this time, too. As either a patient or a loved one, it's easy for you to get discouraged with this process. It helps to know that finding the right meds is not an exact science. But always hang in there, and discuss your frustrations with your therapist or prescribing physician. Your continued persistence to find the right bipolar treatment formula will lead to success.

Finding the Right Medication

Stabilization is marked with two important treatment goals. First, bipolar medications must be noticeably and consistently effective. Collaboration among patient, therapist, prescribing doctor, and family members is essential to achieve this goal. It's often not enough to rely on the patient's subjective report describing how he or she "feels." That can be deceiving for everyone, including the patient. Why? Because stabilization—not just feeling good—is something people with bipolar might never have experienced. And although patients might be familiar with their personal baseline mood zone, they may not be sure how to "feel" within the first few days of medications.

As a therapist, I prefer it when patients don't feel much different than normal in the first day or two because I'm looking for side effects of the medications. I'll discuss side effects in detail later; but for now, know that side effects can appear before the desired effects of the medications. There are exceptions, such as when a person is in a severe manic episode and needs to have dangerous behavior quickly addressed.

If trying to reduce mania immediately, patients can experience the medication as uncomfortable because its chemicals are starting to change the mood—perhaps rapidly. Remember, mania is perceived as a defense against depression. Chemically changing that defense can be scary. In addition, many people with bipolar have experienced this change as a precursor to a depressive episode and it frightens them.

The goal of bipolar medication is to achieve mood stability, but assessing that stability goal can be complicated since it's such an unfamiliar experience. To that extent, a pre-stabilization, symptom-based mind-set is still needed. We continue to focus on individual symptom improvement while we begin to discuss bipolar as a single disorder that has a collection of symptoms. One important way to help assess stabilization is to think of the process as being *less* of something rather than *more* of something. Specifically, we aim for less irritability, less agitation, less depression, less pressured speech, fewer flights of ideas, and so on. By comparison, pre-stabilized people with bipolar tend to look for *more* because that's the manic way of observing themselves and life around them. If you're beginning bipolar medications, don't expect to identify more good things about how you feel on medication—at least not until you meet the stabilization goals.

Time and patience are needed to assess how the medication is working or not working. Please be aware that any fluctuations in sleep, eating patterns, mood, and energy level might be more related to early medication activity than the bipolar disorder itself. These can be the result of side effects or good medication activity that will become more evident as the process continues.

Once the medications are reducing symptoms, no significant side effects are apparent, and the patient and family are working with treatment professionals to maintain a firm medication schedule, the first goal of stabilization has been achieved.

Accepting Bipolar as a Lifelong Mental Illness

In the second goal of the stabilization phase, the patient and family must accept the presence of bipolar disorder and the fact that it's a *chronic* mental illness. Everyone involved passes from denial to acceptance to complete this important phase.

Truly accepting a lifelong disorder requires working through various emotions, including shock, sadness, and anger. It can be easy to *say* you have bipolar disorder, but talk isn't enough. Coming to acceptance requires experiencing a deeply felt truth.

It's difficult to fully *believe* you have a mental illness. And it may be harder for you if you're a family member to accept that forever truth. People are geared toward believing illness is temporary and treatment is a battle to be won. Their desire is to *beat* bipolar, not *own* it. But accepting it starts your personal ownership process. It seems like a long and arduous road at first, but through the stabilization phase, you can discover the journey isn't that scary after all.

Treating the Entire Disorder

Acceptance also means the focus of treatment turns from a symptom-based approach to treating the entire disorder. The components of bipolar are brought together and laced into a single, comprehensive model.

The pre-stabilization phase emphasized the less agreeable symptoms (such as irritability and agitation) instead of trying to convince patients their agreeable symptoms (such as euphoria, increased energy) were problems, too. Moving through to stabilization, the complete disorder is emphasized. Patients can better understand that the desired or pleasurable aspects of bipolar create the more devastating aspects and that one symptom connects with others to form a whole condition.

At this point, we're no longer treating bipolar symptoms; we're treating bipolar disorder.

As a patient in the stabilization phase, you probably have a variety of concerns about treatment. You might worry about what effects medications could have on your body. You might mourn the loss of mania with all its great feelings and excitement. Your feelings as a family member of someone with bipolar can range from hope and optimism to skepticism and doubt. Be assured the opportunity to address your feelings and issues will take prominence soon.

For everyone involved, keep in mind this is the second phase of your long journey into owning bipolar disorder. There's more work to do, but also more achievements to enjoy as you go forward.

Post-stabilization

Post-stabilization is marked by:

- Taking medications for long-term maintenance
- Expecting consistent treatment collaboration
- Treating the whole person
- Accepting a new self-identity

The first two bipolar therapy phases are meant to be short while this third phase is long. That's because post-stabilization represents the rest of the bipolar patient's life after stabilizing. Similar to the way recovering alcoholics are always in recovery, people with bipolar have to manage their lifelong mental illness every day of their lives.

Taking Medications for Long-Term Maintenance

This phase begins with effective, well-managed medications. That means the patient and family members actively collaborate with the treatment professionals about taking meds as prescribed while maintaining regular medication and therapy visits. Some medications, especially lithium, require getting prescribed blood tests. Follow-through on this medical exam is consistent, so any problems with meds can be addressed without delay. A trusted family member can be an excellent support for reminders on taking medications, setting appointments for the doctor and therapist, and making sure that treatment continues uninterrupted. Although a family member can help establish a good medication routine, taking medications regularly is a life adjustment that needs constant attention in the short term. But if you focus on these needs early in the post-stabilization phase, eventually keeping up with medications will be as easy to remember as brushing your teeth. Owning bipolar in post-stabilization becomes a part of life, not the center of it.

A common aspect of post-stabilization is that, eventually, bipolar patients want to get off their medication. Not everyone will try it, but anyone in this phase considers it at some point (or at several points). If you do, it's not a failure. I always let my post-stabilization patients know to expect it. I don't present it as a negative expectation, because again, it's not about failure. It's about what to expect when you're managing a lifelong mental illness.

However, going off meds would likely put you back to a pre-stabilization crisis. An inherent problem with going off meds well into the post-stabilization phase is that you might immediately feel fine and stay in a baseline zone for a long time. This is deceiving for everyone involved. Why? Because you aren't cured. Inevitably that crisis will return and probably arrive unannounced.

I encourage my patients to keep my phone number handy, even if they're doing well and not currently scheduling appointments. I tell them they'll want to try living without meds, that it's part of managing the illness—it's not a failure—and reflects their success to that point. Then I say, "If you ever feel like going off your meds for any reason, will you give me a call first?" I ask my patients; I don't tell them. This is a collaborative approach, implying a need to own their condition and not take orders from the "authority." If they hesitate to agree, I know they're not ready to collaborate on that point. Then I ask why, so we can both understand what's standing in the way of that commitment. Returning to a previous treatment phase, I tell them, is nothing to be ashamed of. You don't have to be perfect to manage a lifelong illness; no human is. But ownership requires reaching out when things take a wrong turn.

I have seen people with bipolar return to treatment after varying degrees of consequences. But when they do return, their passion for bipolar ownership is greater than ever. If they survive the consequences, they find a greater strength to carry on their journey.

This is an excellent reason for you to stay connected with your therapist, whether appointments are frequent (like 2–4 times per month), less frequent (once per month or less), or scheduled on an "as-needed basis" (you call the therapist when you think you need it). Even if you believe that life is fine, there's likely an important issue to deal with in therapy. You may or may not be aware of it, but allow your therapist to help you uncover your current concerns to avoid a bipolar relapse.

Expecting Consistent Treatment Collaboration

Gone are the days when doctors simply handed bipolar patients prescriptions and sent them on their way. Instead, collaboration is key among patients, family members, and treatment teams. This concept is especially important during post-stabilization, since patients and their loved ones take more ownership of bipolar, and stay in ongoing communication with the professionals. This may seem foreign to you, especially if you've always relied on doctors to tell you what to do, and have not felt empowered to offer ideas or informed questions during the appointments. But as you'll see, knowing more about bipolar and what to expect will help you have more productive discussions with your treatment team.

For example, many bipolar patients and their loved ones may discover that a few aspects of the disorder can appear resistant to medication and may not respond well all the time. Changes occur as a result of age, new medical factors, and life stressors, such as relationship, job, or financial losses. An occasional medication review is needed to discuss these issues with the prescribing doctor—all part of the post-stabilization experience. But you don't need to wait for the doctor or therapist to suggest that appointment—you can take the initiative and set up the session before it's mentioned.

And remember, treatment of bipolar disorder is an ongoing process. Everyone must be flexible in the approach to treatment without abandoning it entirely. Whether you are a bipolar patient or loved one, problems that make bipolar care more difficult can make you feel discouraged. But know that there are always answers to the difficult challenges that lie ahead. Later in this book, we'll look at how to thrive in post-stabilization by improving personal health and how to experience success through typical bipolar complications.

Treating the Whole Person

Therapy in this phase moves from treating bipolar disorder to treating the whole person. Goals that were delayed in pre-stabilization can be reintroduced into the overall discussion. For instance, if you originally came to treatment for relationship therapy, but it was interrupted to treat mood swings, now is the time to proceed with a greater focus on repairing your relationship.

However, know that the original presenting complaints in therapy and how the bipolar patient perceives them will be different in this phase. The prism through which people with bipolar see themselves, their loved ones, and the world around them will change as a result of stabilization. For example, there may have been inappropriate outbursts of anger, or casual responses to serious situations when manic. As a patient in post-stabilization, you can now see how your perceptions and inner conflicts had been influenced by an untreated disorder. You can understand more clearly how bipolar disorder can make you say and do things against your better judgment. And you are in a better position to understand how mania and depression permitted unresolved unconscious desires and fears to manifest as chaotic behaviors. Re-examining life from this clearer perspective certainly enhances everyone's experience. But that's not the end of the story.

Accepting a New Self-Identity

In the early post-stabilization phase, people with bipolar often struggle to see themselves through that altered perception. This is called a loss of identity. Knowing they have been bipolar their whole lives, they have only known themselves amid their mood swings. They have only seen themselves as manic (or hypomanic), or depressed, or "crazy at times," or the "life of the party," or "superman/superwoman," and so forth. They have only realized how certain conditions and interpersonal situations have "set them off" into a mood episode. They also remember how productive, creative, and "happy" they were when manic.

The post-stabilized bipolar patient often wonders, *Will I ever get that euphoric feeling back again?* They also fear their loved ones (or future loved ones) will see everything about them as "bipolar." They wonder whether people can trust them, especially if they get emotional in otherwise regular life. And frequently they don't yet trust their own emotions, fearing those awful days and nights of their untreated condition might return.

Establishing a healthy sense of identity is an important goal of post-stabilization. Therapy helps parse those positive aspects of personality and personal aspirations from the bipolar disease process. For example, a young musician believes he can only compose exciting new musical scores when on a manic high. He accepts his bipolar disorder and ongoing treatment but fears he'll never compose at the same creative level. In therapy, he explores his creative abilities and processes to discover new ways to use organizational tools to produce an exciting piece of music.

People with bipolar can come to realize they were letting mania "do the work for them"; they were actually relying on their disease for energy and motivation. They often acknowledge they have to work a little harder but can still find deep inspiration from their newfound journey through bipolar. And without depressive episodes, they can be productive on a more consistent basis.

People with bipolar also discover they can be unique characters, still quirky and fun, intriguing and sexy, without threatening their relationships, jobs, or social standing. During stabilization, patients fear that medications will turn them into zombies, leaving nothing of their coveted individuality. They sometimes believe that psychiatry—with their families as co-conspirators—are out to make them robotic conformists.

During post-stabilization, patients discover that their mood swings—not their own sense of reason—governed their moral and social decisions. They understand they're actually freer to define who they are as individuals and how they want to play out their life stories. They can choose their own paths rather than live in the deceptions brought on by bipolar disorder.

They also become accustomed to more appropriate emotional patterns. When we examined bipolar mood zones, the baseline zone is what most people identify as their "normal" emotional experience. But in life, no one has the exact same "normal" as anyone else.

Living in a baseline zone doesn't mean a bipolar patient won't have periods of joy, sadness, anger, irritability, frustration, desire, "good days," and "bad days." A full life requires a healthy range of emotional experiences. It's useful for patients and families to work through conflicts in therapy. They discover the difference between old emotional patterns governed by bipolar disorder, and new ones that reflect "the real person." During this phase, people with bipolar and their loved ones work to understand what a true emotional life looks like.

If you're a patient entering into post-stabilization, well done! I'm sure you've gone through several tests of your courage, and you have every right to feel good about your accomplishment. Chapter 8 discusses positive ways to improve good health and personal success, which can help solidify your progress and improve your chances for a happy life.

If you're a family member, way to go! Now you can experience your relationship with your loved one in a fresh way. You may still struggle to define life together, but you bring hope and knowledge to achieve lasting success.

CHAPTER 6

The Medication Conversation

THE PROPER TREATMENT FOR BIPOLAR disorder requires medications that reduce the severity of mood swings, bringing daily emotional life closer to the baseline zone and enhancing the chances that psychotherapy will succeed. There's no appropriate substitute for bipolar medications in achieving stabilization. Yet, it's understandable why you may have various concerns or fears about medications, especially if this is your first time considering bipolar treatment, or you've had a previous experience when treatment didn't go well. We've explored how denial can be a defense against fear. Here, we'll begin to confront fears and build confidence in how approaching bipolar medications can be an empowering experience for you and your loved ones.

These drugs are referred to by different terms, which you will read about in Chapter 7, but for now understand that psychiatric medications are chemical compounds developed in pharmaceutical laboratories and typically prescribed for bipolar disorder. Because bipolar is considered a brain-based disease, medications to treat it are specifically designed to target certain functioning systems in the brain. These drugs undergo large-scale clinical testing before they're released for doctors to prescribe. Many have been used for decades by large numbers of people around the world, thus creating an ever-increasing knowledge base on their effects. And this information is used to insure their safety and effectiveness.

But make no mistake: Taking bipolar medications is nothing to treat lightly. Any fears or concerns you have should be discussed in a thorough manner, and without judgment. A substantial part of the "medication conversation" addresses concerns from patients and family members about taking medication. Before we discuss the different bipolar medications and their effects, let's look at how to better overcome problems that can get in the way of treatment success.

Medications: From Fear to Acceptance

When bipolar disorder is diagnosed, the issue of medications inevitably arises; medications are essential to successful treatment. But the medication conversation is one of the awkward moments of the pre-stabilization phase. I often see discomfort, shame, distrust, disbelief, and even anger on the faces of the patients and their families at the mention of medication, and there is a reluctance to continue the discussion. Why do patients and families prefer to avoid talking about medication for this disorder? There can be a number of reasons why anyone would feel this way, some of which I'll mention. But the truth is, they aren't the only ones who might be uncomfortable having this conversation. Some therapists and even prescribing doctors may feel hesitant when introducing the need for a medication. You might think those who frequently treat bipolar disorder would be confident in what they're proposing to patients and families—and certainly most of them are. But treatment providers are people, too, who can have negative opinions about certain drugs or the drug industry itself. Maybe they've had unpleasant experiences with medications with their patients, in their own lives, or with their loved ones. Or perhaps they anticipate resistance to the idea of medications and fear losing their patients' trust.

Discomfort concerning medications seems uniquely prevalent in psychiatry. Many people who claim to dislike the idea of medications when it comes to mental health have little problem taking antibiotics for infections or pain relievers when they hurt. It gets interesting when someone rules out medications to stabilize a mood but opens a bottle of wine or smokes a joint to relax at the end of the day. Humans have had a long and complicated relationship with mood-altering substances. But I think the stigma of mental illness—along with the stigma of getting help for it—makes taking bipolar meds problematic for people.

The word "stigma" means a sign of dishonor or disrepute attached to a person for the purpose of social shaming. Understanding what a person might fear when confronted with the need for bipolar medication requires an appreciation of the concept of stigma. Although modern society has come a long way in understanding psychiatric disorders of all varieties, some mystique around mental illness still pervades. Before science could explain mental illness as the result of genetic or neurological issues, people believed dark, mystical forces caused it. A person who fell into epileptic seizures, for example, was thought to be possessed by a demon. Someone with schizophrenic hallucinations was accused of being a witch. And what about a person with bipolar disorder and psychotic mania?

Picture life in a village during the Middle Ages when clinical psychology or brain science didn't exist. There's a villager who perpetually avoids contact with others (depression). But one night, witnesses see a figure who looks like that man running naked through the woods, barking loud and making incoherent sounds (psychotic mania). It was just dark enough for witnesses to see hairlike shadows on his body and hear noises sounding like a powerful animal. The next day, the village elders convene and conclude he's a werewolf.

For centuries, popular folklore like this example attempted to explain what science had not yet revealed. The resulting bias for those who were mentally ill was devastating. They were generally thought to be evil pariahs who had committed grave sins to suffer such fates. At times, they became scapegoats, meaning others projected onto them their own wrongdoings to feel better about themselves. They were routinely cast out. Later in history, they were warehoused in asylums and often abused. Rampant shaming often condemned the mentally ill to a life of indignity.

Even today, certain cultural and family biases against mental illness and treatment can't be ignored. In some cultures, individual flaws are viewed as objects of shame onto the whole family and even a broader community. As I stated at the beginning of this book, you do not have bipolar in your life because of anything wrong with you as a human being. You are definitely not a beast, or a pariah, or meant to be a scapegoat. If you've ever felt anything like this, it's because of the history of stigma. Indeed, many people now know that mental illnesses—including bipolar disorder—aren't the products of bad behavior, sinfulness, or anything shameful. They know that people with bipolar are not possessed by evil spirits or meant to be scapegoats for the sins of others. And yet, in spite of what's known about this genetic brain disorder, remnants of shaming from the tragic past can be present in the world around us and make it more difficult to get treatment.

To counter these feelings, an open discussion among trusted individuals about having bipolar disorder can help you feel that you are simply a person who's dealing with a problem in life, just like anyone else who's facing trying times. When we avoid these conversations, we tend to feel alone in the world. The best conversation includes others who can reduce shame and inspire hope.

And yet, as much as you may worry about what a diagnostic label of bipolar disorder can mean in your life, you may be even more afraid of what it means to take the medications for bipolar.

Perhaps the diagnosis alone seems less threatening. You can more easily dismiss the diagnosis because it's largely theoretical—a "label" you can ignore, especially if you're hanging on to denial. Once you've put a pill inside you, however, it's as if there's no turning back. It's a tangible action that means you are "officially mentally ill." It brings home the reality of confronting the inner feeling of shame that's been carried through many generations. This is why I've heard some patients say, "I don't want medication because it means I'm crazy."

On the surface, that's twisted logic because bipolar has been present long before getting treated for it. But deep down, "crazy" means "ashamed." Despite our "enlightened" modern sensibilities, it still may be difficult for you not to feel like a flawed outcast who is rejected by society, even condemned. In that case, you could be less concerned about the untreated behavior and more concerned about how treatment is viewed by others. It's as if having to take medication exposes the bipolar disease—and the perceived shame—within you.

Ted's Story

After years of suffering bouts of depression broken by periods of manic instability, Ted finally came to meet me for a bipolar evaluation. Initially, Ted had a difficult time accepting that his mood swings were actually a mental disorder, because mania had previously yanked him out of apathy and low productivity, especially at the office. But when a coworker noticed Ted was acting erratic and discourteous with customers on the phone, he pulled Ted aside and said it was time to get help.

Through the pre-stabilization phase of therapy, Ted began to accept his bipolar symptoms. But when it came to medication, Ted still showed resistance. "I can't do that," he said. "What if my boss finds out that I'm taking meds for bipolar? She'll probably want to fire me." I pointed out that his boss wouldn't know if Ted takes meds if he chooses not to tell her. In fact, that's confidential information and illegal grounds to terminate someone.

What was really happening was that he felt great shame attached to taking medication, and was projecting his shame onto someone else—his boss. But the ironic thing is that Ted's untreated bipolar could create far more suspicions and a greater likelihood of putting his job at risk. Denial tries to convince the patient the untreated behavior isn't wrong; the stigma says the medications will reveal the shame within.

Worrying about how others might see you as a person with bipolar can bring up inner fears of rejection and abandonment. Thus, having a meaningful conversation about stigma and shame is key to making the overall medication conversation meaningful.

The biggest problem with stigma is the avoidance of treatment. Whatever it takes for you to address stigma and overcome feelings of shame, embarrassment, guilt, and cultural biases are absolutely necessary for stabilization and lifelong treatment success. And a good place to do it is in therapy.

Treatment fears in general are neither completely rational nor irrational. Most fears have elements of both, at least in terms of their origins. That's likely because we're flooded with information at an unprecedented level. With so much thrown at us, how can we sift the real from the imaginary? Concerns can be based on misinformation. Perhaps you've known others who had problems with medications or heard horror stories, even if they have no factual basis. You may have a history of sensitivity to certain medication, or have family members who've had similar problems.

Understanding the struggle with accepting bipolar disorder and taking medication for it potentially requires a process toward collaboration and acknowledgment. But as you proceed, you come to discover that there is no shame in getting treatment, and that you are truly one of many who share in the bipolar journey. As actor Catherine Zeta-Jones said, "This is a disorder that affects millions of people, and I am one of them. If my revelation of having Bipolar II has encouraged one person to seek help, then it is worth it. There is no need to suffer silently, and there is no shame in seeking help."[1]

Models of Treatment

A doctor with a white coat, stethoscope, and clipboard was once the ultimate authority who stood above his or her patients and told them what to do. The patients "complied." Perhaps they asked how best to comply, but they weren't allowed to question the doctor's judgment. Whether the doctor's persona was kind or stern, the patients' behavior toward treatment was based on the compliance model of treatment. This model is quick, easy, and simple in theory. The doctor diagnoses a problem and dispenses medicine. The patient takes the medicine and comes to follow-up appointments.

Thankfully, many physicians today realize this model never worked well and is outdated and unrealistic. What would typically happen? Because of their hesitation, patients would verbally agree to go for a med consultation but never make an appointment. Or maybe they'd go and receive a prescription but never get it filled. Or maybe they'd get it filled but never take the medication. Or maybe they'd start taking it and then stop. They may have every conscious intention to comply with the treatment, but because they grew up in the compliance model of treatment and never knew anything else, they don't fully address their concerns with the expert.

On the drive home from a doctor's office, have you ever thought of questions you should have asked during the appointment? Did it feel like the session went too fast, even though at the time you just wanted to get out of there? Did you consider calling the doctor with questions but didn't, for fear of looking stupid? Having been accustomed to compliance, patients can agree to things too quickly and rush away from the situation, like teenagers facing authority figures. This is the central problem with the compliance model; it doesn't encourage *owning* bipolar.

I propose a twenty-first-century model.

The barrage of information, fears around mental illness, and the essential need to take full ownership of bipolar demand adopting a different approach—the collaborative model of treatment. This is a model that invites cooperation rather than demands it. It's a standard of care that allows time and opportunity to ask questions, express fears and concerns, and to be heard without judgment. It's a way that allows for family to get involved, too.

When patients and/or families are in denial about bipolar disorder, they're not noncompliant; they're simply not ready to collaborate. If they believe bipolar exists in their lives but question the need for medication, they're closer but not completely ready to collaborate. If there are substantial disagreements among the patient, the family, and the medical providers, collaboration won't occur.

So, what to do?

During the pre-stabilization phase, it's natural for fractures to exist among everyone involved in your treatment. Entering the stabilization phase, the aim is to close those fractures and solidify as a working team. This demands the best that each person can contribute. And guess who the team captain is? It's not the doctor, the therapist, or the family member. It's you, the bipolar patient. All the other members can be in place, but the team does not advance as one unit until you decide it's time to collaborate and bring the team together.

For everyone involved, it's important to have room to start the collaboration at your own pace. In therapy, I engage patients until they signal their readiness. After medication *fears* are fully explored, greater understanding and motivation for treatment replace those fears. This leads to greater *interest* in medications, which results in better adherence to the collaborated treatment plan.[2]

This work is not outside psychotherapy; collaboration is a big part of therapy because it explores inner fears and works through denial toward bipolar acceptance. When you are ready to collaborate, you'll likely find the psychotherapy experience highly productive, even with discussions that have nothing to do with bipolar and its medications. Additional trust in the therapy process—as embodied in the short term by the collaborating therapist—comes from a collaborative effort captained by you, the patient. The table is then set for more therapy achievements during the stabilization phase and through post-stabilization.

Evelyn's Story (continued)

Here again is Evelyn. She discovered her bipolar diagnosis and acknowledged the need for medication, but she also understands that it is only the start of changing her life.

> I went to my doctor, and after much discussion, we agreed this was more than depression. The mood swing, rages, outrageous behavior, the inability to control myself... something else was going on here.
>
> There were other manic behaviors: incredible bursts of energy, extreme emotions and I was unbelievably euphoric! No matter what happened, I'd just laugh. And there was so much going through my mind all at once; I didn't have enough time to get it all out.
>
> The highs were amazing. I didn't want them to end. Everyone liked my highs. But the lows were bad, very dark and deep—no one would want to be around me then.
>
> So I started taking medication. The doctor said it wouldn't completely get rid of the highs, just take them down a bit. He said it would help me not get depressed and would stabilize the mood swings to avoid the mania. Let me tell you, it has saved my life!

I won't lie: I do miss the "high" highs. I don't get like that anymore. But I don't get the lows that often. The meds didn't completely fix the problem. I still need to do my part. I need to find the triggers and do my best to avoid them. Yes, bipolar disease still affects my life, but I'm doing a good job managing it. I won't let bipolar control my life![3]

Notes

1. Cotliar, S., & Tauber, M. (2011, May 2). Her private struggle. *People*, 75(17). Retrieved November 30, 2014, from http://www.people.com/people/archive/article/0,20484164,00.html
2. Shea, S. C. (2006). *Improving medication adherence.* Philadelphia: Lippincott Williams & Wilkens, 37–40.
3. Pipich, M. (Ed.) (2013). The bipolar network's shared stories. Retrieved December 1, 2013, from http://bipolarnetwork.com/shared-stories.html

CHAPTER 7

• • • • • •

Bipolar Medications

To UNDERSTAND BIPOLAR MEDICATIONS IN general, it's essential to learn about lithium first. It's one of the naturally occurring elements on the periodic table you might have learned about in high school chemistry.

Lithium was first proposed for use in the nineteenth century as a treatment for seizures, anxiety, and mania. However, it was nearly forgotten until European scientists brought it back for research during the 1940s and 1950s. In the 1970s, it was approved in the United States for the treatment of bipolar disorder. Although every new drug seems to be the latest miracle drug, lithium indeed was a breakthrough. Even today, it's considered the initial treatment of choice for mania.[1] That's why it's often referred to as the "gold standard" of bipolar medications.

Discovering that bipolar was relatively easy to treat with lithium inferred the disorder was neurological and genetic in its foundations. Because many bipolar patients seemed to improve with a medical treatment that stabilized brain activity in a way that talk-based psychotherapies couldn't accomplish, many professionals thought that exploring psychological issues in bipolar disorder was unnecessary. But we know now that the meds-only approach to bipolar treatment is grossly deficient. With meds only, people don't receive comprehensive therapy to work through all the barriers to successful bipolar care.

Besides, the meds-only approach doesn't promote collaboration. Instead, it represents a compliance approach, and as I mentioned, this doesn't work as well in the long-term. In fact, some might even find the approach dictatorial. Can you imagine if you were told, "My job is to get you on meds!" Your reaction would be understandably defensive, probably with the pushback of denial. Because bipolar patients are expected to present a certain degree of denial, working together as a team in treatment not only reduces denial, but improves successful medication outcomes. And beyond taking medications, it's critical to pursue the real work in therapy to create a healthy, productive life.

Today's approach combines appropriate medications and psychotherapies involving patients and families. This provides a comprehensive, collaborative model that has the potential to fulfill the need of *owning* bipolar.

With that in mind, this chapter focuses on understanding the specific medications for bipolar disorder and what to expect from them. I believe that becoming familiar with these medications can reduce the avoidance of using them. You may find some of the following information a bit technical, but know that having proper knowledge can empower you in this critical aspect of life-long care.

Note: All medication-related information presented in this book is for the purpose of understanding available treatments for bipolar disorder so individuals can be supported in seeking proper care. It's not meant to replace medical information and recommendations from a physician. Patients and families are encouraged to seek specific answers applied to their circumstances from the right medical specialists.

Medication Effects: What to Expect

What to look for with bipolar medications can be broken down into two simple categories:

1. Main effects
2. Side effects

The *main effects* of a medication are hoped-for results and unexpected improvements. Basically, any reduction of a bipolar-related symptom that brings a patient closer to the baseline zone could be considered a main effect. For bipolar specifically, meds can be more antimanic or antidepressive, or used for long-term maintenance. (Note: I use "antidepressive" for anything that improves the depression side of bipolar. "Antidepressant" refers to a specific class of drug. Therefore, an antidepressive effect may come from a medication that isn't necessarily an antidepressant.)

Depending on several factors, certain bipolar meds have fairly balanced antimanic and antidepressive actions. However, bipolar patients with a recent or current manic episode often start in the pre-stabilization phase with medications known to be antimanic, which calm symptoms down toward the baseline zone. If the current or more recent mood episode is depression, then beginning bipolar meds known to have an antidepressive effect are often preferred. These meds tend to be less sedating and can lift up a mood toward the baseline zone with less chance of becoming a catalyst for mania.

The *side effects* of a medication refer to unwanted results that don't reduce bipolar symptoms. However, common side effects can occur in any medication used and generally are considered acceptable when they're short-lived or produce minimal inconveniences. Common side effects are usually also considered mild rather than moderate to severe. For example, dry mouth is a common side effect of a med. To overcome it, a patient may be instructed to increase hydration, especially for the seventy-two hours after taking the medication. This kind of common side effect resolves itself as the body gets used to the drug, although it can reappear if the dosage is increased.

Uncommon side effects ranging from mild to severe require greater attention than common side effects. They can cause the prescribing physician to reduce the drug dosage or switch to something else. One uncommon, yet important, side effect of mood stabilizers is skin rash, which should be immediately brought to the doctor's attention. (See "Reference Guide to Bipolar Medications" at the end of this book.)

New patients and families typically do their own medication research and find a litany of side effects for any drug. Some of them can be downright scary! It's always good to bring these concerns to the attention of the treatment team. When people have a collaborative discussion about side effects—both common and uncommon—they frequently discover that, although they can be serious, side effects are usually manageable and rarely produce long-term harm.

Remember, owning bipolar ultimately refers to patients taking control of their treatment. Even if certain side effects aren't a big deal to others, they might be to you. Having an open dialogue about medications in general and side effects in particular is a vital step in the ownership process.

Most prescribing doctors start a medication at the lowest dose appropriate for the patient and the severity of the presenting symptoms. A standard treatment philosophy is to increase medication dosages until patients reach the maximum level of main effects while maintaining the minimal level of side effects. Adding one or more meds to the overall treatment plan when certain symptoms appear resistant to the initial meds, is also typical. In addition, certain meds can be replaced or eliminated when it's apparent they're no longer necessary.

Medication needs can change as patients move through the stabilization phase of treatment, but when they progress into post-stabilization, medications are set for long-term maintenance and relapse prevention. At that point, it's not unusual for them to be more antidepressive than antimanic. This makes sense when you think about mania as a defense against depression. Once mania has been reined in sufficiently, preventing the depression side of bipolar disorder becomes a good defense against mania in the future.

However, patients during post-stabilization can report feelings that resemble the start of a manic episode. These should be discussed with the physician, who might recommend resuming a medication that's more antimanic than antidepressive or increasing the dosage of the current one. In this scenario, know that changing meds doesn't change the course of psychotherapy. However, it can be a good opportunity for further exploration into the person's life and overall disease process. If mood swings can be well managed medically as the individual deals with challenges, then therapy discussions can help them work through tough situations without returning to a full pre-stabilization crisis.

Common Types of Medications

A simple list of bipolar medications and their main and side effects is available in the "Reference Guide" at the end of this book. You may want to explore the guide as you read the following sections. Although several types of medications are used to treat bipolar disorder, the most common ones are addressed here in four groups:

1. Mood stabilizers (lithium and anticonvulsants)
2. Antipsychotics

3. Antidepressants

4. Antianxiety/anxiolytics

Mood Stabilizers

This generic term is meant to signify what this type of medication can do for bipolar patients specifically. Basically, mood stabilizers are lithium and several drugs designed for the treatment of seizures. They're known as either anticonvulsant or antiseizure medications.

These medications, and especially lithium, have represented a revolution in treating bipolar disorder. Why? Because they help the brain regulate mood states without the risk of becoming manic catalysts or creating undue sedation that can worsen depression. Mood stabilizers can also be given with other psychiatric medications to enhance the stabilization process by targeting specific symptoms, including psychotic ones.

How lithium works in the brain isn't fully understood, but this elementary substance is believed to act similarly to other chemicals involved in the conduction of nerve cells in the brain.[2] Simply put, the brain runs a complex series of electrical currents that allows for messages to move throughout the brain and the entire central nervous system. An electrical charge goes through a nerve, which passes a chemical message to another nerve, which has a charge go through it, then passes the message on to the next nerve, and so on. Due to its steady properties, lithium stabilizes this conduction process across different areas of the brain, while preventing radical changes that could produce mood swings.

Anticonvulsants work in a similar way. They essentially calm brain activity, especially in brain areas that can overreact, such as in epileptic seizures. Certain anticonvulsants such as divalproex or carbamazepine can be more antimanic than antidepressive while others, such as lamotrigine, can be more antidepressive.[3] Some work well with mixed bipolar episodes,[4] which include rapidly shifting euphoric or dysphoric mania with depressive symptoms. Anticonvulsants are prescribed singularly or with another med in this or another class.

Lithium by itself is balanced enough to be both an antimanic and a maintenance drug, and it has been shown to significantly decrease the risk of suicide during long-term use.[5] When switching from initial doses to maintenance doses, lithium is usually decreased and kept at a lower level for the long term. The body processes lithium by way of the kidney instead of the liver, making it a potentially good choice for those who have a history of liver disease.

With lithium being the gold standard bipolar med with all these good properties, why would people with bipolar need anything else? As is true for any bipolar medication, not all patients respond to lithium the same way. There's no way to predict how someone will react without trying it first. A few of my patients on lithium have reported not feeling much of anything for several days, which isn't a bad way to start. Others have reported feeling a little strange, or feeling "spacey" and "out of it" within the first few days. Some of those patients will improve but those who won't are switched to another mood stabilizer.

Many patients tell me "a fog has been lifted" within a few days of their lithium treatment. Some even have said they've experienced a sense of "normal" in their lives for the first time. The sudden change in homeostasis (balance) it creates can be new and refreshing.

However, lithium has inherent problems, usually associated with how it needs to be taken and managed by the patient. With lithium, there's a "therapeutic window" for the main stabilizing effects to occur. If the lithium level in the blood is too low—below the therapeutic window—it can't do its job. If the level is too high—above the therapeutic window—moderate to severe side effects can occur. When patients begin lithium treatments, they should have blood-serum samples drawn according to their doctors' requirements.[6] There's no way around this. They might need several blood samples taken and verified over time until the lithium levels are clearly within the therapeutic window and there's confidence those levels will remain constant.

Drawing blood is an obvious problem for those who are deathly afraid of needles. It can exacerbate the difficulties of making and keeping lab appointments for blood tests. Getting patients to agree to take meds in the first place is difficult, and then comes this undesirable procedure in addition to it. Also, certain changes in routines such as increased exercise can affect lithium levels, so dosages must be monitored to accommodate the changes.

As a result, many doctors—although approving of lithium in general—avoid prescribing it when they don't have confidence in a patient's level of collaboration. Failure to keep up with the needs of lithium treatment through post-stabilization can have serious consequences. Thus, it might be easier for them—and their patients—to turn to other bipolar meds that don't require initial or repeating blood tests.

If you have no reservations about following through with a successful lithium treatment, let your doctor know. Physicians can be creatures of habit, reflexively going with what they know. Getting all the information you can ahead of time and then presenting ideas and questions during the medication consultation increases your results and shows a sense of *owning* bipolar.

It's possible your physician finds your unique profile of bipolar symptoms better suited to an anticonvulsant, though bear in mind, divalproex and carbamazepine also have therapeutic windows that require some attention. No matter what your first medication may be, keep two things in mind. First, unless you have a strong, unpleasant, or unexpected reaction, be willing to allow the mood stabilizer time to work properly. Usually two to three weeks is a good benchmark. Second, feel free to ask your doctor why you received this particular med instead of others in its class. Remember, asking questions doesn't mean you're unco-operative. Rather, it demonstrates your knowledge, commitment, and willingness to collaborate on treatment.

Antipsychotics

First made available in the 1950s, antipsychotic medications were found to be effective in treating schizophrenia. The early "major tranquilizers" also reduced mania, but they had strong side effects, such as involuntary muscle movements and slurred speech, especially when used long term. Today, doctors often pre-scribe a second generation of these medications known as atypical antipsychotics. They have fewer side effects than the ear-lier generation in treating bipolar disorder.[7] This is particularly good for patients whose mood events include psychotic features, seen in the most severe forms of mania and depression.

Antipsychotics can be quite effective as antimanic agents, and they can be used with other bipolar medications depending on the individual's need. Antipsychotics can also be prescribed for bipolar depression. At times, certain ones are paired with an an-tidepressant to avoid becoming a catalyst for mania. Physicians sometimes turn to antipsychotics to even out mixed episodes of mania and depression[8]—at least until a more identifiable mood pattern takes form. Although they may be used for bipolar with-out psychotic symptoms, these medications help reduce agitation, delusional or paranoid thoughts, and hallucinations that accompany psychotic mania or psychotic depression.

I have noticed a number of physicians turning to antipsy-chotics when they are not sure about a bipolar diagnosis in a given patient. When uncertain about bipolar, they may feel more comfortable treating patients with these medications, since some symptoms cross over with other disorders that are treatable with antipsychotics. This may be particularly true for severe depres-sion when bipolar is suspected because they won't induce mania.

Antidepressants

These include:

- SSRIs
- SNRIs
- Atypicals
- Tricyclics
- MAO Inhibitors

Neurotransmitters thought to be associated with depression, namely serotonin, norepinephrine, and dopamine, are increased—or made more available in the nervous system—with the use of antidepressant medications.[9] This is believed to work overtime as a way to improve moods in many who suffer from depression.

Confusion can become rampant when taking antidepressants for bipolar disorder, however. Most antidepressants do well in the treatment of non-bipolar major depression and dysthymia, but they can act as manic catalysts in people predisposed to bipolar disorder. As a result, antidepressants alone are not recommended as a treatment for bipolar depression.[10]

Although antidepressants certainly have antidepressive effects in most people, for people with bipolar in particular, they may have an excessive effect. Antidepressants given by themselves have been shown to increase the risk of mania, while antidepressants provided with a mood stabilizer did not increase that risk.[11] In fact, if an antidepressant medication alone results in the first manic or hypomanic episode of the person's life, the diagnosis is likely bipolar disorder.[12] This can account for situations when misdiagnosed people with bipolar—especially young people—start an antidepressant and become more agitated, more hyperactive, or more suicidal than before within the first few days of taking the drug. Some people react poorly to drugs of all types, but these peculiar reactions to antidepressants can act as a diagnostic for bipolar.

Although antidepressants can create problems for bipolar patients, they can be useful by maintaining an antidepressive effect in some bipolar patients. This is usually in conjunction with an antimanic agent that keeps a lid on mania. But because there are antidepressive alternatives for bipolar patients that won't induce mania by themselves, having an antidepressant such as an SSRI or SNRI paired with an antimanic would usually occur after other options were attempted.

Note: Dysphoria can present a common misunderstanding with medications. Dysphoric mania, marked by high irritability, can be confused with the irritability and agitation accompanying major depression, making the manic and depression mood zones difficult to distinguish. Indeed, that's an understandable error. But it's another reason why it's important to get a comprehensive evaluation and history along with viewpoints from other professionals to accurately distinguish mania from depression, especially if you recognize these symptoms yourself. I've known patients in dysphoric mania who received an antidepressive bipolar medication and the result was greater agitation! When they received a medication that was more antimanic, the irritability and agitation lowered and stabilization followed.

Antianxiety/Anxiolytics

Typically, these medications are effective in relieving mild to severe anxiety in many circumstances. Other medications may take anywhere from a few days to a few weeks to achieve full effect, but antianxiety meds work within minutes to calm nervous system functioning. Their immediate benefit can help reduce irritability and excitability, especially in dysphoric mania. They can also aid sleep. While they are not intended to replace other bipolar medications, doctors often use antianxiety meds in conjunction with antimanic ones.[13]

The more common antianxiety agents such as alprazolam, clonazepam, and lorazepam are the only bipolar medications known to be habit forming. Patients who use these medications over an extended time run the risk of dependency.[14] (One exception is buspirone, which is considered non-addictive.[15]) For bipolar treatment in general, taking an antianxiety med can help control some manic symptoms along with reducing early signs of anxiety—that is, until the full effect of mood-stabilizing medications take hold.[16] Doctors often prescribe these meds for a brief period but don't necessarily continue their use for long-term maintenance. If used long term, they're often provided on an "as needed" basis to reduce occasional bouts of anxiety.

KEEP IN MIND that prescribing physicians have several options to treat patients in various conditions. Psychiatrists in particular usually follow specific paths of logic. They start with one or two medications, for example, and proceed to others depending on the results along the way. These logical paths are known as *algorithms*.

At the top of the bipolar medication algorithm is what's called a first-line treatment. A first-line medication for mania could be a mood stabilizer such as lithium or divalproex, or it could be an atypical antipsychotic. If only one drug is introduced at the first line, it's called monotherapy.[17]

If that's not going as well as hoped, for whatever reasons, doctors go to a second-line treatment. This can involve changing the medication in monotherapy or combining meds. Third-line and below may involve additional medications, including older types of antipsychotics, antidepressants, and so on. Similarly, a first-line bipolar medication for a recent episode of major depression could start out as a mood stabilizer (lithium and/or lamotrigine) or a different antipsychotic in monotherapy. The second line could involve combinations to improve mood without the risk of inducing mania.[18]

The fundamental points are these: Doctors have alternatives at their disposal, and patients should understand what to expect from their medications. It's often necessary to explore several options while navigating through the stabilization phase of treatment.

More About Side Effects

Through years of practice, I have seen bipolar patients benefit from all of these categories of medications with few significant problems. However, among the various side effects there are a few that many people find objectionable, sometimes to the point of discontinuing meds on their own. Those side effects include:

- Intestinal distress (nausea, constipation, diarrhea)
- Dizziness
- Tremors (especially in the hands)
- Weight gain
- Sexual dysfunction
- Just not "feeling right"

Mild intestinal distress, mild dizziness, and mild tremors usually resolve within the first few days of medication use. If they stay mild but don't resolve, the prescribing physician might replace the meds for something more easily tolerated. If they get worse—especially with lithium or anticonvulsants—the physician should be contacted immediately, as these can be signs of toxicity (above the therapeutic window).

But even though these side effects are typically well managed, sensitivity to meds in general and the perceived stigma of bipolar meds in particular can result in a patient ending treatment without investing the time to work through these problems. Immediate signs of discomfort can confirm the patient's conviction that meds are bad or not worth the trouble.

One side effect often discussed with patients is weight gain. For some, this side effect can be a deal breaker. Because weight gain is not experienced immediately, patients already are well into their treatment before it becomes an issue. But once the pounds start piling on, they become concerned.

Weight gain is a common side effect for lithium and a few of the anticonvulsants, antidepressants, and antipsychotics. This is a problem for many patients, especially those who have a history of obesity before bipolar disorder became a problem. The effect of weight gain on self-image and overall health can threaten any early enthusiasm to get on meds for lifelong treatment, but not all meds produce weight gain, so a physician can prescribe something else.

Many of my patients stopped medications because of weight gain, but they didn't give that as a reason. This tells me they didn't want to stop the medications but instead were feeling ashamed about the weight gain and didn't want to discuss it. If you're worried about weight gain or experience it, there's nothing to be ashamed of. Talk to your doctor. There are other options. Having an open dialogue with your doctor about all of your concerns empowers you to take control of your treatment, stick with the overall program, and achieve successful stabilization.

It's also wise to complete an overall health assessment when medications are initiated. This can provide a preview of how you will adjust to meds in general but also identifies positive changes in diet and exercise. Feel free to ask about clinical dietician or nutritionist referrals, which could be useful in properly managing this issue.

Similarly, you may feel reluctant to discuss sexual problems, including those caused by bipolar meds known to suppress sexual desire and/or performance in both men and women. Several patients have mentioned the irony of getting along better with their intimate partners as a result of medication but not feeling as sexual toward them.

This can be resolved by switching to other meds known to have fewer sexual side effects. But without a thorough discussion about the issue, patients sometimes stop the meds or make adjustments that complicate their overall care. For example, some patients may intend to stop meds when they want to have sex. The rationale is that once they've been intimate, they can return to their bipolar care. But switching back and forth—for any reason—can seriously impair the medication's effectiveness, especially in the long term.

Although it may feel awkward, discussing your concerns about sexuality throughout treatment is critical to maintaining lifelong collaboration.

Just not "feeling right" is not an official side effect of medication, but it's a common complaint that patients often can't articulate any better than that. If your first feelings on bipolar medication are difficult to express, don't worry. That's not unusual. Stay in touch with your doctor, and allow for further conversation about which side effects are at play. You will likely feel better within a few days, but it's good to have an open discussion to keep treatment going until you reach stabilization.

Pregnancy and Breastfeeding (Lactation)

Taking medications for bipolar disorder is often discouraged during pregnancy and breastfeeding. This poses problems for any bipolar woman who relies on them to stabilize her mood swings. Research on bipolar medications with both pregnancy and breastfeeding is limited because of ethical considerations. Some options to maintain treatment may be available under the close observation of your treatment team. For example, switching to a low-dose antipsychotic during pregnancy may be considered, while certain antidepressant medications might be permissible during breastfeeding.[19]

These are personal decisions to be made between the patient and doctor. Stopping bipolar medication on your own when you are trying to get pregnant or immediately after you find out you are pregnant can be risky. Not only must you contend with life off the meds, but altered hormones and the stress of a major life-changing event can have an effect on your mental health. Talk to your doctor about the best options for you. Work together to monitor any changes in mood and together make a plan to insure the safety of both you and your baby.

Often bipolar women won't breastfeed their babies so they can return to treatment as soon as possible. This can be necessary especially for women who have suffered postpartum depression or postpartum mania in the past. But a woman's decision to breastfeed is personal, even for a new mother with bipolar disorder. It should be decided ahead of time, ideally when you're still on medication and in your best state of mind. You want to make decisions when you are as stable as possible, with no impairment due to being off meds.

Preparing to go off meds requires loving support from family and friends, especially if the pregnant bipolar woman is to become a single mother. I suggest putting in place a well-coordinated plan involving the patient, family, and treatment team—including the patient's obstetrician and pediatrician—as soon as possible.

Use of Alcohol, Marijuana, and Other Recreational Drugs

Recreational drug use is a key issue when bipolar medications are introduced. For patients who have a history of addiction to any substance, it's vital to have a combined therapy approach focused on both bipolar disorder and addiction recovery. This is true even when the excessive drug use occurs only during manic and/or depressive episodes. Both approaches can be regarded as one treatment because the bipolar disorder likely drove the addiction process and vice versa—inadequate bipolar therapy could have resulted in substance abuse relapse.

Alcohol

Alcoholism commonly occurs with bipolar disorder at high rates, even higher than with major depression.[20] However, many bipolar patients don't have a defined pattern of addiction. For example, they may have enjoyed social drinking most of their lives, even if they've had a few instances of excess. When taking bipolar medications, they wonder whether mixing alcohol with meds could be a problem. But they won't always ask. And even if they do ask, they don't always get a straight or consistent reply.

For some patients, the thought of giving up a glass of wine with dinner or a couple of beers with the guys seems too difficult. Treatment professionals might offer advice from several viewpoints, in part to avoid scaring bipolar patients out of taking medications. They discuss limiting alcohol consumption when on bipolar medications because it can interfere with the drugs' effectiveness or perhaps complicate liver functioning.

If you do drink, I encourage you to have an open and honest conversation about alcohol use with your doctor and therapist. Let them know what your usual drinking is per day or per week. And let them know if you've had any history of alcohol abuse, or "problem drinking." A clear conversation will ultimately help to make stabilization effective.

Here's something also to think about: As much as people associate alcoholic beverages with having a good time, alcohol is a depressant. The "good time" usually comes from alcohol suppressing your inhibitions accompanied by an immediate relaxation effect. But consider what it could mean to add a depressant to your bipolar treatment plan, at least to levels that could confound becoming stabilized. I strongly encourage my patients to avoid alcohol through stabilization to get an accurate assessment on how the meds are working. After that, occasional or limited drinking can be discussed as long as they've not had a discernable problem with alcohol in the past. In many instances, however, patients decide to quit drinking entirely. They choose to avoid anything that could potentially interfere with their newfound stability.

Marijuana

Marijuana has a unique place in the bipolar medication conversation because particular properties in marijuana require a more careful examination. One is the active ingredient in marijuana, tetrahydrocannabinol (THC), which is responsible for the psychological effects of "being high." These effects include feelings of well-being and mild-to-moderate euphoria, along with relaxation.

Marijuana also can produce therapeutic effects without the withdrawal symptoms that accompany other recreational drugs. Think about recreational marijuana and that giddy, elated feeling comes to mind. But for bipolar patients who use marijuana, the story doesn't end there. Marijuana possesses many different chemicals collectively known as cannabinoids of which THC is only one. Another is cannabidiol (CBD), which possesses an anticonvulsant property and recently has shown to dramatically help some children suffering from epilepsy.[21] More research is needed on CBD's potential as an anticonvulsant/antiseizure medication, and also in treating bipolar disorder. It makes sense that THC isn't the only chemical that attracts bipolar patients. Remember that anticonvulsant medication is a first-line treatment for bipolar. The CBD content also may provide a key therapeutic effect that makes marijuana desirable for people suffering mood swings.

When I address marijuana use with bipolar patients and their families, I suggest the patient may have used it for self-medication, even if that wasn't the conscious intention. I could make that argument for any recreational drug, but it seems especially true in this case. Marijuana users often tout its benefits from a medicinal standpoint anyway, and presenting the information about CBD helps put their using it into proper context. It also removes from the conversation any prejudice that all users are just "stoners" intent on avoiding life's responsibilities.

I believe long-term marijuana use can affect energy, motivation, and ambition, but understanding an individual with bipolar disorder means appreciating the need to medicate in whatever way seems most effective. That's why I encourage patients to consider medications that are better researched for mood stability than marijuana. More research on the positive psychological potential for marijuana—CBD specifically—is required before it can be used routinely for bipolar disorder. Anecdotal evidence is important but only to guide that research. If marijuana use is a part of your life, having a frank dialogue that presents facts and an open mind to marijuana's potential benefits may help you feel less guarded and more respected. In that spirit, you, your loved one, and your treatment team can also explore other medications in a collaborative way.

Cocaine, Heroin, and Meth

Drugs that possess a severe potential for addiction, including methamphetamine, cocaine, and heroin, pose a great danger. It can be hard to imagine people using these hazardous substances as self-medication, but in the context of bipolar disorder, it's not a stretch. These drugs result in a flood of dopamine in the brain, which produces an intense euphoria similar to mania. A person using them in a manic state is attempting to multiply and extend the euphoric effects, even to hazardous levels. The depressed person is searching to replicate that manic feeling without having to wait for the brain to produce it on its own.

But when dopamine levels in the brain are dramatically increased, a downward crash follows the upward spike. The cyclical nature of addiction is made worse by bipolar disorder, but the overwhelming desire is to feel better than the desperate feelings brought by depression and, in the case of severe addiction, the dreadful feelings of withdrawal.

In the case of past or recent drug use, hiding that truth is understandable. If this applies to you, feelings of shame are to be expected. But know that your bipolar treatment can be very helpful in maintaining sobriety and lifelong health for you and your family.

Opioids

This discussion also needs to address opioid medications, typically prescribed for pain relief. These drugs include morphine and others that mimic morphine. They are important for people who medically need them, but require close management by a physician. Even then, getting addicted to them is possible. If you've taken opioid drugs for self-medication and/or recreation, there are significant consequences including addiction. If you're a bipolar patient who suffers chronic pain, you certainly may need these pain medications for daily functioning, but still feel free to discuss the potential for addiction with your doctor. Some good news is that you might also benefit from mood-stabilizing and/or antidepressant medications that can also relieve pain. In such cases, collaborative treatment involves a pain-management specialist who appreciates the connection between physical and mental health. Discussing these options with your treatment team can reduce the potential risks when using opioids.

With exceptions such as pain medications, many doctors won't prescribe bipolar medications until there's reasonable certainty their patients have abstained from any of these substances for a time. That's a tricky thing because the sooner bipolar patients start mood-stabilizing meds, the better chance they have to avoid a substance abuse relapse.

But proper treatment requires clear understanding of the medication's main effects and side effects, which can be complicated by other drugs interfering. Moreover, there can be physical risks with too many competing substances in the body at once. That's why a period of sobriety is needed before bipolar medications can be started and assessed for effectiveness.

Even then, there's no guarantee of immediate success. Some mood stabilizers help reduce withdrawal symptoms from alcohol and treat alcohol abuse along with bipolar.[22] But the best treatment plan won't replace what it feels like to be high—and not depressed. This is especially true because bipolar meds take days to weeks before their full effects are realized.

This is a good example of how "just getting on meds" is inadequate. The necessity of psychotherapy, and staying connected with your treatment team and supportive family members through a complicated stabilization phase, creates the best opportunities for long-term success. This is especially true while waiting for the right medications to do their job.

Steven's Story

Steven, an adult on mood-stabilizing medication for bipolar disorder, reflects on his early methamphetamine use this way:

> There was immediate gratification with the meth. I would just feel normal. It was like a miracle cure. I don't think I was conscious to the fact that I was using it because I felt so awful. I just wanted to feel normal and that's what it did. I didn't realize I was self-medicating. I thought I was just doing it because all of my friends were. But now I realize that it wasn't just about wanting to have a good time. There was an underlying issue I was dealing with— bipolar disorder.[23]

Children and Adolescent Patients

There is often controversy about young children having bipolar disorder. Research shows it does exist in children and adolescents, but there's also a need to further clarify symptoms and treatment in these young patients.[24] Remember that a person from day one can have the genetic predisposition for bipolar, and certain catalysts can occur anytime to bring out the symptoms. The problem with diagnosing kids in general is that their behaviors could point to any number of mental health problems, not only bipolar. But it doesn't mean we can rule out bipolar disorder altogether.

Concerns about bipolar medications intensify when the patient is a minor. It's common for parents and some professionals to immediately question the need for meds. Would they do more harm than good? One common fear is medications that target brain chemistry will cause brain damage and specifically long-term personality and functional impairments.

However, research shows the opposite might be true. Untreated mood swings in any patient can result in the persistent reduction in needed brain chemicals and brain cell volume. Bipolar medications are described as having "neuroprotective effects," which means they prevent these problems, thereby protecting the brain from long-term damage and perhaps even working to reverse damage.[25] These benefits are particularly important in young people for the same reason many people fear medications—that the onset of bipolar disorder frequently occurs during a critical time in a person's brain development. If treatment is delayed in young bipolar patients, however, brain damage could have deeper, longer-lasting consequences. As in all mental health problems, early detection and treatment provide the best chance for success, especially for kids with bipolar disorder.

Another common issue involves the dosages of medications relative to adults. In prepubescent children, their increased metabolism affects how meds are approached. It's not unusual for dosing guidelines to come close to or equal adult dosing.[26] Parents sometimes worry that adult doses for kids seem like overkill, and a few might cut the prescribed doses themselves. This can result in real problems, because young people process these medications through their bodies a lot faster and more efficiently as they approach puberty. Without enough medication circulating before the body eliminates it, potential results are diminished. The treatment team won't know what should be done next, especially if doses were arbitrarily decreased without consultation.

Taking a careful approach to initial dosing makes sense for any patient. But keep in mind that children, including adolescents, may need higher levels of medication than you'd imagine. And likewise, more time and patience are needed to allow treatments to work effectively. (See Chapter 11 for further insights on bipolar children and their parents.)

Elderly (Geriatric) Patients

Many medical issues often converge in an elderly bipolar patient. It's a fact of modern life that the older we get, the more medicines we take. A common concern for elderly bipolar patients involves the interactions of bipolar meds with other medicines they take. This doesn't have to be complicated, but it often is for two reasons:

1. Elderly patients can lose track of all the medications required each day.
2. Communication among medical providers may not be adequate, especially if they rely solely on their patient's report.

Having assistance from a family member or case worker can help ensure patients are taking their meds as prescribed, but the assistant must also provide updated information to the professionals involved. Attending medical appointments with the patient is ideal, but sometimes just sending information by fax or email to the doctor's office is sufficient. It's important to get information releases so everyone involved can communicate with each other to prevent a serious medical crisis for the bipolar patient.

Aging presents new challenges for even the most cooperative bipolar patient. Just as we have to account for increased metabolism in young patients, we have to adjust to decreased metabolism in elderly patients.[27] If they used lithium for many years, it may have to be switched because the kidneys, which can decline with age, process it. Also, side effects and increased sensitivity to all bipolar medications become more problematic over time, along with other medical issues.

At the same time, depression itself is a common disorder among elderly people, and contributes to increased suicide potential and mortality from other medical disorders.[28] It's important to remember that just because an elderly bipolar patient is not manic doesn't mean he or she may not be living in a depressive mood zone. Along with body changes and medication adjustments of all kinds, the treatment team must remain vigilant to mood changes that could threaten the patient's overall health. (See Chapter 11 for further discussion.)

Other Bipolar Medical Treatments

For most bipolar patients, finding the right combination of medications can take time and require a great deal of patience. Eventually though, patience pays off and the medication plan is successful. However, there are occasions when doctors try many different bipolar medications in different combinations without consistent success, especially when bipolar depression has been very severe and hard to treat over a long period of time. When various trials of medications don't produce good results over time, other medical options for bipolar treatment can be considered. Two of those choices are electroconvulsive therapy (ECT) and repetitive transcranial magnetic stimulation (rTMS).

ECT

ECT is a medical procedure considered by many to be effective in cases when antidepressant medications fail at every turn. But despite its pretty well-documented effectiveness and relative safety, some still find the procedure too radical, and perhaps even barbaric. Controversies about the use of ECT usually come from the rather disturbing images of ECT in the past. Many people still remember the 1975 movie *One Flew Over the Cuckoo's Nest*, where Jack Nicholson's character, Randle, was forced into ECT, causing him to writhe and convulse violently. And for what? His unruly behavior in the mental ward.

This is not at all what ECT looks like today. It is not used to control personal behavior, but to offer a viable treatment approach in the most difficult cases of severe depression. In present terms, ECT is only considered after different treatments have been used and exhausted. It is not forced on psychiatric patients, but is available to offer relief when nothing else seems to work. Additional psychiatrists are usually brought in to assess patients for ECT appropriateness. And like most medical procedures, the patient's informed consent is typically necessary to proceed.

ECT is performed by a trained physician while the patient is under general anesthesia and muscle relaxants. Electrodes are placed on the patient's head, and an electrical current is passed through the patient's brain, intentionally causing what is essentially a brief, purposeful seizure, which the patient doesn't feel. After the treatment, a period of rest and recovery is provided, and the patient typically experiences short-term memory loss and confusion. The desired main effect is to change the patient's brain chemistry to improve bipolar symptoms, particularly depressive ones. In addition to some confusion and memory loss after treatment, patients may also experience side effects of nausea, headache, jaw pain, or muscle aches.[29] Several of these treatments are typically applied over days or weeks to help stabilize symptoms in a consistent manner.

If your doctor has proposed the possibility of ECT, know that it's been shown to be effective in improving depressive symptoms without becoming a manic catalyst or threatening long-term mood stabilization.[30] You can take your time and discuss the pro-

cedure with your team, and perhaps you may also want to speak
with others who have had ECT treatments. Remember, even if stabilization has been difficult, you can still own bipolar by
evaluating your options freely.

rTMS

rTMS is a noninvasive medical procedure that uses a magnetic
field around the patient's brain, using the same type of magnetic
fields used in MRIs. There's no need for anesthesia or sedatives.
An electromagnetic coil is held over certain areas of the head, and
pulses are emitted. With rTMS, the objective is to stimulate nerve
cells in a way that can improve depressive symptoms. Patients require a series of these treatments, typically a daily dose over
several weeks. It is generally considered to be effective for major
depression. Though patients usually don't feel discomfort during
treatment, it can cause the side effects of headaches, scalp pain,
or general discomfort around the treatment area afterward. There
is some concern that noncontrolled seizures could happen, but
this is apparently uncommon.[31]

For bipolar disorder, rTMS may be a viable alternative treatment when trials of bipolar medications have not worked well or
consistently. A review of some research on rTMS suggests that it
may be effective and safe in treating bipolar depression without
the threat of becoming a manic catalyst.[32] So while you can certainly discuss this option with your doctor, know that more
studies on rTMS are likely needed to confirm its place as a standard treatment for bipolar disorder.

Herbal Remedies

Concern about medications leads some people to pursue herbal
or "natural" remedies. Alternatives to treatments outside of what
the Food and Drug Administration (FDA) approves and what

licensed physicians would prescribe are unacceptable for bipolar disorder. Some physicians might add certain vitamins or other supplements to complement bipolar medications, with the goal of enhancing performance and improving overall health. But taking supplements in lieu of medications isn't appropriate for bipolar.

One herbal preparation in particular, St. John's Wort, gets attention because it is believed to relieve depressive symptoms similar to antidepressants. Some people try it as an alternative to prescribed meds, but taking it outside a doctor's care for bipolar disorder isn't advised.

There are case studies suggesting that St. John's Wort can become a catalyst for mania.[33] In addition, the FDA does not regulate St. John's Wort, so there can be variations in actual dosages from one preparation to another. In addition, approved medications typically have greater predictability in their main and side effects than herbal remedies. This is due to extensive controls in production and testing.

I suggest staying under the collaborative care of the bipolar treatment team and ask all the questions you need to establish your confidence in the overall plan. Straying from standards of care may be intriguing but ultimately could have consequences you'd regret.

Notes

1. Preston, J. D., O'Neal, J. H., & Talaga, M. C. (2013). *Handbook of clinical psychopharmacology for therapists* (7th ed.). Oakland, CA: New Harbinger Publications, 197.
2. Ibid. 202–203.
3. McElroy, S. L., Keck, P. E., & Post, R. M. (Eds.). (2008). *Antiepileptic drugs to treat psychiatric disorders.* New York: Informa Healthcare USA, 379–384.
4. Konstantinos, F. N., Kontis, D., Gonda, X., Siamouli, M., & Yatham, L. N. (2012). Treatment of mixed bipolar states. *International Journal of Neuropsychopharmacology, 15*(7), 1015–1026.

5. Baldessarini, R. J., Tondo, L., Davis, P., Pompili, M., Goodwin, F. K., & Henne, J. (2006). Decreased risk of suicides and attempts during long-term lithium treatment: A meta-analytic review. *Bipolar Disorders, 8,* 625–639.

6. Preston, O'Neal, & Talaga. *Handbook of clinical psychopharmacology for therapists,* 199.

7. Hirschfeld, R. M., Bowden, C. L., Gitlin, M. J., Keck, P. E., Suppes, T., Thase, M. E., et al. (2010). *Practice guideline for the treatment of patients with bipolar disorder* (2nd ed.). Arlington, VA: American Psychiatric Association, 9.

8. Konstantinos, Kontis, Gonda, Siamouli, & Yatham. Treatment of mixed bipolar states, 1015–1026.

9. Preston, O'Neal, & Talaga. *Handbook of clinical psychopharmacology for therapists,* 179.

10. Hirschfeld, Bowden, Gitlin, Keck, Suppes, Thase, et. al. *Practice guideline for the treatment of patients with bipolar disorder,* 10.

11. Viktorin, A., Lichtenstein, P., Thase, M. E., Larsson, H., Lundholm, C., Magnusson, P. K. E., & Landen, M. (2014). The risk of switch to mania in patients with bipolar disorder during treatment with an antidepressant alone and in combination with a mood stabilizer. *American Journal of Psychiatry, 171*(10), 1067–1073.

12. American Psychiatric Association. (2013). *Diagnostic and statistical manual of mental disorders* (5th ed.). Washington, DC: Author. 124–125.

13. British Psychological Society (2006). *Bipolar disorder: The management of bipolar disorder in adults, children and adolescents, in primary and secondary care.* Leicester, UK: Author. 207–208.

14. Ibid.

15. Preston, O'Neal, & Talaga. *Handbook of clinical psychopharmacology for therapists,* 215–217.

16. Hirschfeld, Bowden, Gitlin, Keck, Suppes, Thase, et al. Practice guideline for the treatment of patients with bipolar disorder, 42.

17. Crismon, M. L., Argo, T. R., Bendele, S. D., & Suppes, T. (2007). *Texas medication algorithm project procedural manual: Bipolar disorder algorithms.* Austin, TX: Texas Department of State Health Services. 7–12.

18. Ibid. 8-12.

19. British Psychological Society. *Bipolar disorder,* 33–37.

20. Sonne, S. C., & Brady, K. T. (2002). Bipolar disorder and alcoholism. *Alcohol Research and Health.* Retrieved September 24, 2016, from http://pubs.niaaa.nih.gov/publications/arh26-2/103-108.htm

21. Gedde, M. M., & Maa, E. (2013). Whole cannabis extract of high concentration cannabidiol may calm seizures in highly refractory pediatric epilepsies. American Epilepsy Society annual meeting, Seattle, WA. Abst. 3.330.

22. Sonne, & Brady. Bipolar disorder and alcoholism.

23. Pipich, M. (Writer/Director). (2013). Excerpts from friends from the bipolar network sharing their stories about living with bipolar [Radio series episode]. In M. Pipich (Producer), *Breakthrough with Michael Pipich*. Phoenix AZ: VoiceAmerica Network.

24. Renk, K., White, R., Lauer, B-A, McSwiggan, M., Puff, J., & Lowell, A. (2014). Bipolar disorder in children. *Psychiatry Journal*, 928685.

25. McElroy, Keck, & Post. *Antiepileptic drugs to treat psychiatric disorders*, 390–391.

26. Preston, O'Neal, & Talaga. *Handbook of clinical psychopharmacology for therapists*, 253.

27. Hirschfeld, Bowden, Gitlin, Keck, Suppes, Thase, et al. Practice guideline for the treatment of patients with bipolar disorder, 25.

28. Reynolds, C. F., Cuijpers, P., Patel, V., Cohen, A., Dias, A., Chowdhary, N., et al. (2012). Early intervention to reduce the global health and economic burden of major depression in older adults. *Annual Review of Public Health, 33*, 123–125. Retrieved September 25, 2016, from https://ncbi.nih.gov/pmc/articles/PMC3356692

29. Mayo Clinic Staff (2017, May 9). Electroconvulsive therapy (ECT) risks. Retrieved June 28, 2017, from http://www.mayoclinic.org/tests-procedures/electroconvulsive-therapy/basics/risks/prc-20014161

30. Perugi, G., Giorgi Mariani, M., Toni, C., & Medda, P. (2015). ECT in bipolar disorder: It can be considered a mood-stabilizing treatment? *Brain Stimulation, 8*(2), 417.

31. National Institute of Mental Health (2016, June). Brain stimulation therapies. Retrieved June 30, 2017, from https://www.nimh.nih.gov/health/topics/brain-stimulation-therapies/brain-stimulation-therapies.shtml

32. McGirr, A., Karmani, S., Arsappa, R., Berlim, M. T., Thirthalli, J., Muralidharan, K., & Yatham, L. (2016). Clinical efficacy and safety of repetitive transcranial magnetic stimulation in acute bipolar depression. *World Psychiatry, 15*(1), 85–86.

33. Kaustubh, J. G., & Faubion, M. D. (2005). Mania and psychosis associated with St. John's wort and ginseng. *Psychiatry (Edgmont), 2*(9), 56–61.

CHAPTER 8

• • • • • •

Thriving in Life After Stabilization

WHEN PEOPLE ARRIVE AT POST-stabilization, they can experience emotional relief along with a sense that life has given them a second chance. But the journey into good mental health isn't over. It's only just begun. Following the grief over the loss of the old identity that was attached to bipolar mood swings, people with bipolar now struggle with a new identity that requires an improvement in lifestyle to protect and enhance their well-being.

Here are some positive ways to improve good health and personal success while staying vigilant to potential threats to stability during the post-stabilization phase. It's vital to maintain awareness of any threats to mood stability, which can appear from various life circumstances. Furthermore, life in post-stabilization does not have to be boring, as so many people with bipolar also fear. This chapter will help you attend to your health needs while reducing the chance of a return to pre-stabilization by:

- Finding your rhythm
- Understanding the creative process

• Attaining your goals
• Managing negative life events

Finding Your Rhythm

Finding your rhythm includes some very typical things but cannot be overlooked when maintaining stability and learning how to thrive. This involves three very important factors: diet (nutrition and weight management), exercise, and sleep.

This first part may not sound so interesting, because who hasn't heard that they should do better with diet and exercise? And sleep seems to be obvious, but at many times also seems impossible to improve. It may be tempting to just skip this part of owning bipolar. But I assure you, these are the areas that, if neglected, can easily overcome the great work of getting to post-stabilization. Let's look at these factors as they apply to bipolar disorder, both to make sure they don't become threats to stability, and ultimately to help you thrive in a healthy, happy existence.

When it comes to diet and exercise in treating bipolar disorder, the key focus is moderation. Just as you work toward a baseline zone from a mood perspective, your diet and exercise patterns should also be in a consistent zone. Remember that people with bipolar have seen themselves and the world around them in extremes. They've often treated diet and exercise in the same way. Behavior and personal choices in both the depressive and manic zones can result in self-neglect and the consumption of junk food and junk drink that throws off the body's homeostasis.

However, it's not unusual for manic or hypomanic individuals to exercise or diet with extreme purpose, which can also threaten homeostasis. While they have neglected good health practices in depression, they feel so energetic in mania that they suddenly become full-time experts in all things healthy! Their quest for health looks more like an obsession to find the Fountain of Youth, and the resultant changes in attitude and appearance can be dramatic—even destructive. After a period of laying around feeling sad and slothful during depression, ideas of a massive weight loss, black belt in a martial art, or a triathlon gold medal becomes the unstoppable objective in mania.

In post-stabilization, a moderate approach to diet and exercise promotes a healthy and balanced lifestyle. It serves the body, yes, but also keeps the mind focused on patience and long-term planning to meet all post-stabilization goals.

Now that doesn't mean that competitive athletes with bipolar should abandon intensive training routines. Instead, athletes at all levels should consider their personal goals and how to attain them in a consistent manner that doesn't put stability at risk. And this is a good therapy topic to explore to accommodate all changes in the lifestyle of a person with bipolar. Staying consistent in interpersonal, occupational, and recreational routines is central to maintaining post-stabilization success.

I believe that every bipolar patient needs to address diet and exercise with their physician and therapist, ideally during the stabilization phase in preparation for post-stabilization. Eating the right foods, including fruits and vegetables, whole grains, and lean proteins, is essential, especially when taking certain bipolar medications that can increase weight. Positive changes in exercise are necessary, too. But physicians need to be apprised of changes in lifestyle, even the good ones. That's because any changes in activity level can alter med concentrations in the body, especially with lithium. Lithium as a salt is sensitive to changes in activity levels and metabolism. Thus, an initial discussion about these lifestyle factors with the treatment team can create an important foundation for post-stabilization health, and the continuing discussion through post-stabilization will help maintain stability through the process.

Discuss an exercise and diet plan with your treatment team. If you need more specialized help, consider a specialist, such as a certified dietician. This conversation should include ideas for specific physical activities and timeframes for those activities.

Investigate within yourself and through discussion what you'd like to do, and how much time per day and week you can dedicate to it. Try to be as specific as possible. Examples include, "I'd like to walk the dog every day for a half-hour, then do some weightlifting for fifteen minutes." Or, "During the summer, I'm going to ride my bike on that trail by my house, three evenings a week." Also consider social activities, such as lightly competitive team sports or group exercise classes, where people encourage each other and promote both fun and accountability to achieve healthy goals together. Moderate goals keep things sustainable and life-giving, while reducing the potential for manic involvement, which can be excessive and even dangerous.

Likewise, dieting shouldn't be boring or isolating. Encourage family and friends to join in cooking and eating healthy and interesting foods. Instead of having social events centered exclusively around alcohol, try other means to increase fun and accountability to what ultimately encourages stable, but enjoyable experiences. Patients and families can collaborate together to improve everyone's health habits.

But it's not just what you do for a balanced, moderate approach to diet and exercise. It's also about what you avoid doing in the extreme. Namely, sugar, caffeine, nicotine, and alcohol.

Sugar, caffeine, and nicotine act as stimulants, and alcohol is a depressant. We've discussed alcohol already, but it's important to limit your intake of stimulants as well, even milder ones like sugar and caffeine. That's not to say that a patient in post-stabilization can't enjoy cake and coffee from time to time. It means that a moderate approach will minimize a person's reliance on these stimulants to keep energy and motivation levels high. An increase in stimulants can become catalytic for mania.

Nicotine is a highly addictive stimulant. It's found in all tobacco products, which are known to cause life-threatening diseases. Like other addictive stimulants, many people with bipolar seek tobacco for a dose of nicotine because it provides a sudden increase in dopamine in the brain. Depressed people can find some relief with it, while manic people can extend their sense of pleasure. In post-stabilization, nicotine can improve feelings of well-being that individuals have lost through stabilization. But more commonly, they may find certain bipolar meds—especially antimanic ones—make them less energetic, and seek nicotine to bring them "up again."

It's important to limit the use of mild stimulants, and eliminate nicotine. Compromising on a healthy diet to take in more stimulants, or high caloric/low nutrient junk food, can mean that a person with bipolar is headed in the wrong direction. It's not enough just to say to yourself, "Oh, it's okay to cheat on diet and exercise once in a while." It's better to look at these as possible signs of trouble, and ask, "I've been working well on staying healthy and in my baseline zone. What's going on now that could be changing my approach?"

Keeping a good approach to diet and exercise is about moderation, which doesn't mean you have to be perfect—just as consistent as you can. In doing so, you lay a foundation in finding your rhythm. Rhythm in music is the steady beat by which all other facets of a song—like the melody and harmony—can follow the pattern and stay together to its completion. The other parts of a song can be unique, but they're unified by that constant rhythm. In the same way, people with bipolar can be as unique as a one-of-a-kind melody, but still need a steady beat to keep going forward.

That brings us to a very important component to finding that rhythm: the very basic, and often abused, need for sleep. Recall that decreased need for sleep is a symptom of bipolar mania and hypomania. People in a manic mood zone will often defend their lack of sleep as no problem, while their energy and motivation are at maximum levels. In the post-stabilization phase, patients generally find the need to sleep, but may have different opinions and feelings about what sleep now means to them.

This mostly comes from the manic idea that sleep can actually interfere with work and creative output, along with feeling that sleep just burns valuable time to accomplish as much as possible. That may be hard to believe for someone who can't possibly function without a good night's sleep, but people with a lifelong history of bipolar can relate. The old adage "I can sleep when I'm dead" could have been coined by a bipolar patient. However, in the new identity discovered through post-stabilization, sleep becomes one of the most precious assets in life success.

And when it comes to healthy sleep, the concept of rhythm takes on greater significance. Sleep is governed by what is known as the circadian rhythm, which refers to how living creatures operate and respond to the daily, twenty-four-hour cycle. Our brains have internal clocks that function by internal cues and external ones, including light and darkness. Circadian rhythm can keep the body in good functional balance, and is foundational in keeping in sync with the world around us. Sleep not only refreshes and promotes physical healing, it is fundamental in keeping the brain properly regulated, for its own health and its ability to further regulate all body systems.

When we frustrate that circadian rhythm by not sleeping consistently over an extended period of time, we impair the brain's ability to stay in homeostasis. We know that mania usual results in a decreased need for sleep, which in turn throws other systems out of balance as well. But just as mania reduces sleep, reduced sleep can increase the potential for mania. This is an extremely important factor to keep in mind throughout post-stabilization. Poor sleep habits may be the most important factor in bipolar symptom relapse, and good sleep may be the most important preventative factor available, aside from medication.

Most bipolar patients in post-stabilization would rather sleep well than not. They will usually agree that they need sleep, and will often try their best to keep a good schedule of rest. This typically means between seven to nine hours per night for adults, and more for adolescents.[1] And it should be consistent. We can't really make up for lost sleep all the time, or "bank sleep" one night just to "pull an all-nighter" for another. Mood regulation requires brain regulation within the twenty-four-hour circadian rhythm cycle.

But the demands of life can easily get in the way of proper, consistent sleep. Deadlines at work or school, worries and stress from the day or the day ahead, sickness or anxiety, or variable shift work at one's job, can foul real attempts to stay within a good pattern along with fun times, parties, or late night discussions with best friends. Very occasional lapses from your sleep requirements may not be a big deal. But if sleep isn't consistent, thorough and restful, you will be in immediate risk of a manic relapse.

Unintended sleep disturbances, which we identify as insomnia, should be addressed quickly in therapy and with medication to improve sleep if necessary. This usually means that something important is troubling the mind, and needs to surface in therapeutic discussions so the underlying problem can be resolved. Lifestyle choices to stay up late on a regular basis need to be addressed quickly in therapy, as well. There may be something troubling the person, but the response here suggests a significant risk for mania, or that mania might already be surfacing. Therapeutic discussion about what may be disturbing sleep is crucial, along with a medication review. Adding a medication that can aid sleep can be a very useful tool in overall bipolar treatment.

Bipolar patients and loved ones should always pay attention to sleep needs and never take them for granted. I've known many people who talk about their chronic lack of sleep as if it's no big deal, or even something to be proud of. Many spend years of their lives never sleeping properly, and just accept it as a way of life. They may have no idea how they're taking years off their life span. No one can really afford to live life without sleeping well. For bipolar patients, it's an especially critical part of lifelong care.

A life balance that emphasizes good diet, exercise, and sleep provides the basis for better relationships and occupational and recreational opportunities. Energy that comes from healthy sources stimulates the mind and body to do more healthy things and make life-sustaining choices. In harmony with these posi-

tive choices, you as a bipolar patient or family member can find
your own rhythm.

Understanding the Creative Process

One of the biggest concerns I hear as a therapist treating bipolar
patients is the fear they will not be able to create and produce
without manic energy. While medications improve their stability,
they are not accustomed to working, playing, and developing
ideas and projects without the fuel of their upswings. Their intense self-confidence and the belief that anything is possible
when manic—known as hypercreativity—are perceived to be permanently threatened by mood-stabilizing medications.

But through the course of therapy, people with bipolar typically discover that they can return to their jobs, their beloved
creative outlets, and even new and exciting opportunities for their
futures. And they can achieve without the "benefit" of mania.
First, it's important to discuss how creativity can be rediscovered
and harnessed within the bipolar individual—that special talents
are not lost, just separated from manic energy. Then, we can move
toward understanding how to attain personal goals while minimizing the risk of a bipolar symptom relapse.

Let's first take a look at what creativity is. Simply put, creativity
is the ability to perceive things and situations as more than what
they already are, and express those perceptions in particular ways.
To say that someone is "very creative" usually implies they've
taken great steps to develop and refine a craft, and express it beyond the ordinary. Or maybe we witness someone who can blow
us away with some kind of performance, and we say, "Wow, she's
really gifted!" It's true that some people are more in touch with
their abilities than others, but it doesn't mean that the rest of us
can't find our own skills and nurture them through creative
means. When we think of a creative person, we may have an
image of someone like a painter, sculptor, composer, novelist,

fashion designer, chef, or choreographer. Certainly, those individuals can express their creativity quite openly and with exceptional skills. But anyone can act creatively just by envisioning a different manner to approach a problem. For example, you can be more creative in how you schedule your daily activities, or how you interact with others. In family therapy, I always encourage participants to think and act more creatively in approaching communication and problem-solving challenges within their relationships. And when it comes to functioning at work, even if you think you have the most boring job in the world, chances are you can try to be more creative at it, and elevate its place in your life. But no matter what we do in life, creativity expands our thinking to find improved ways to solve problems and feel rewarded for our efforts.

But where does creativity actually come from in the person with bipolar? We have already noted that many great, creative individuals have had bipolar disorder. Thus, it's simple to assume that creativity actually comes from bipolar itself, not from any other source in the brain. But I don't believe that's true, because there are several factors that go into creativity. Various aspects of the brain are involved in creativity, and together they can follow a complicated sequence of mental functions over time. Much of what can be developed can surface from deep within the unconscious, and then sorted through at the conscious level of mental activity. It often takes a stream of thought and emotional experience, as well as education, practice, and sheer focus to produce something creative. That's why it's called the "creative process."

I believe it's absolutely necessary to encourage people with bipolar to view their overall creative process as mostly independent of their mood swings. Mania and hypomania provide energy and expanded self-confidence to push their ideas and projects forward at an accelerated rate. But this is quite different from the origins of the creative idea and its practical purpose. And for that matter, the reckless nature of mania can actually sabotage an otherwise intelligent pursuit.

One simple way to look at this process is with an automobile analogy. Think of the operation of an automobile as involving three things: the engine, the driver, and the fuel. For an automobile to move with a purpose, to go in a particular direction, it needs those three things to be functioning well and working together in harmony. Without any of those pieces in place, you go nowhere.

A successful creative process is like that. Here, the engine is the brain—healthy and stable. The driver is the consciousness of the healthy person, with organization and vision to see the voyage from origin to completion. And then there's the fuel: a consistent pool of energy from a well-kept body, which includes a steady sense of passion and emotional stability to keep the engine and driver moving in the right direction to the right goal.

In untreated bipolar disorder, the fuel is mistaken for the driver, and the machine is run into the ground. People with bipolar confuse mania as the only thing that drives the creative process, having ridden roughshod over proper planning and vision. It overtakes the will of the individual who can execute the right course for all that's needed to get to the goal. Now, mania may be an awesome fuel. But filling your car's gas tank with jet fuel will destroy the engine. It needs the right concentration of chemicals to keep it going at just the right speed for a long, sometimes bumpy, but ultimately successful journey.

It's often difficult to convince bipolar patients that they can retain their special talents and develop a creative process that's healthier for body and mind, but still effective. They're not used to being patient through the process. That's partly because they've always relied on mania to be the creative process in its entirety without any further development of it. Mistaking the fuel for the driver means they can experience a wild ride of imagination and even perceived success at times. But without a steady will and healthy brain to make it function consistently.

And it's also difficult in part because they may have been depressed, believing their previously amazing ideas are now totally worthless. But isn't that a part of the whole process, too? Who hasn't endeavored something really important without self-doubt, or for that matter, criticism from others? We all have to learn a method to manage the "down times" or "blue periods" of our creative processes. We all need to learn when doubt from within and criticism from others is either constructive and needs to be included in our process, or destructive and needs to be withdrawn from it.

Hypomania alone can support hypercreativity, but it's usually associated with having more intense positive emotions, which stimulate the overall creative process. Recall for a moment that hypomania and major depression are needed in the person's history to be diagnosed with Bipolar II. People who move in and out of the hypomanic mood zone, without ever moving into the major depression zone, can likely sustain periods of hypercreativity during their lifetime. But people who suffer periods of intense negative emotions, such as in major depression, often find their superior sense of creativity unsustainable for the long haul, since various factors necessary to complete projects easily fall apart. For people who've suffered Bipolar I, hypercreativity in the manic zone can be grandiose and overly idealized beyond the limits of the person's skill level or social acceptability. This is even truer in the psychotic mania zone, where the individual may be in a delusional state when talking about or acting on hypercreative ideas.

For anyone living in a baseline zone, there can be times when creativity just seems unavailable. They search within themselves for meaning and inspiration, but come up empty. It's tempting for someone grasping for creative juices to decide that this is the time to try life without meds. They don't always plan to give up meds forever; maybe just for a little time to get something important finished. But as we have learned, this can lead to serious consequences.

If you're a bipolar patient, it's understandable that medications may seem to blunt energy and motivation in the stabilization phase. Yet, you might be encouraged to know that a complete and sustainable creative process will emerge through post-stabilization treatment objectives. We know that long-term bipolar therapy is usually geared to prevent depression, which impairs creativity, no matter what your particular situation is. Also remember that bipolar medications have neuroprotective effects from the potential damage of untreated mood swings. Over time, these mood swings can cause neurological impairments, which would deteriorate the creative process. So, to maintain and enhance the creative process, full participation in bipolar treatment can keep your brain—your most important piece of machinery—in good shape for a long, productive lifetime.

Now that we understand more about the creative process in bipolar disorder and bipolar treatment, we can better examine how to attain your life goals in post-stabilization, while reducing the threat of bipolar relapse and a possible return to a pre-stabilization crisis.

Attaining Your Goals

As bipolar patients transition from stabilization to post-stabilization, they are typically anxious to move forward with life. However, as we've discussed, they previously have only seen themselves and life around them through the lens of bipolar disorder. Living in that condition meant believing ultimate success could only be achieved with a manic or hypomanic approach to completing valuable goals. Likewise, avoiding depression meant holding on to that same manic energy as a guard against stagnation and feelings of defeat. In therapy, changing that bipolar lens to seeing self and life through the lens of stability and homeostasis requires a new organizational structure. This section will explore how to develop better plans to attain your life goals.

Goal attainment is very important to post-stabilization patients. Feeling a sense of accomplishment in life helps to solidify bipolar acceptance and the gains already made in treatment. But before I discuss how to build on those gains, there is something you must bear in mind.

There is research to show that bipolar patients are at risk for recurrences of mania when they've experienced successful goal attainment.[2] This seems particularly true after bipolar patients experience smaller successes, as if early success can whet the appetite for bigger rewards. People with bipolar, even in the post-stabilization phase, tend to have more of a need for rewards compared to people without bipolar, likely because the bipolar brain developed with greater need for stimulation in those reward centers.

What this means is that when bipolar patients experience some level of personal success, that good feeling of internal reward can later result in a manic relapse. Since they typically need more reward stimulation, they intensify the need, rather than simply being satisfied with the attainment of a more modest and immediate goal. An incentive that's meaningful to a particular person with bipolar can begin a chain of internal events that could become catalytic for mania. But even without those symptoms during the process toward goal attainment, a person with a history of bipolar could relapse *as a result of attaining that goal!*

This can sound much like someone with a gambling compulsion. Rather than just enjoying the pleasant feeling of a modest win at the racetrack, the compulsive gambler keeps multiplying his bets, seemingly unable to stop the betting, and eventually losing far more than taking the initial reward home with him. The reward itself increases the sense of confidence to keep the activity going, which in turn increases more reward sensitivity. It's a cycle that's hard to interrupt, especially when the individual is trying to recapture the buzz he felt after the first win.

Because bipolar patients, families, and their treatment professionals all want to see success in the new realm of bipolar management, it's easy just to promote and celebrate a patient's goal attainment without much follow-up. It's tempting to say, "Hey, you made your goal, so congratulations!" And then be done with it. But while the rest of us can feel satisfied in the attainment of a particular goal, bipolar patients may be experiencing a cascade of feelings and desires, like a falling row of dominoes that has no perceivable end. They may then feel much like that gambler, ready to parlay their modest winnings for a bigger score, which becomes the manic catalyst they were initially trying to avoid. Therefore, in developing a healthy strategy for goal attainment in the post-stabilization phase of bipolar therapy, it's vital to have an open discussion about both the patient's means to a given goal, *and* how to further discuss and manage feelings after the goal is attained.

In starting a fresh goal attainment strategy, I prefer helping patients identify what their values are, and what they hope to accomplish in the more immediate future. While there is often much emphasis on personal relationships as we've seen in this book, this is a good time to explore occupational and recreational goals under the new treatment needs. Beyond repairing the damage that bipolar has caused to one's life, we look into the immediate future to move toward a thriving existence.

Let's take an example of someone whose bipolar had seriously impacted their standing within their place of employment. There was some important repair work during the early post-stabilization transition, but now the job standing is improved and it's time to build on that success. So, we have Sylvia, who received notice that there is an opening in another department, which would present a new opportunity to move up in her company as a supervisor. Since she is well into the post-stabilization phase of bipolar treatment, Sylvia recognizes that this is an opportune moment, and that she should apply for the new position.

But more than having her application accepted, she's informed there will be interviews conducted inquiring into her technical knowledge and leadership philosophy. She knows now she must take the next week to prepare for this challenge, but she's also aware of how preparation for this challenge could pose a threat to her stability. She's already identified two particular risk factors. How the increased salary can be the sole focus of her manic energy, and how she can sacrifice sleep and nutrition during preparation.

To begin her goal attainment, she must conduct an inquiry into her life values. She can use her therapy for this important process, or share it with a trusted family member. The first set of questions she should ask herself include: "Why do I want this position?" "How does this fit into my new lifestyle?" "How would it benefit me?" "Will it present new stressors?" "How will those stressors affect me and my loved-ones?" "How will I manage an increased salary?" These questions can slow down any possible impulsivity to just dive into the goal, and instead encourage serious thought into the meaning of the goal. If the answers lack substance or sound a bit hollow, it's probably good to review her life values again before entering the challenge.

Next, she'll begin an organizational plan for interview preparation. In the past, Sylvia would easily forgo a simple schedule, in favor of scattered hours without proper rest and refueling. She recalled her college years when she often "crammed for tests," staying up late at night and working all the next day. Now she understands the need to pace herself. She consults with her therapist and a family member on how to divide the hours per day and evening, then she'll write down an outline for each time frame, and stay within those limits to insure proper rest and recovery. Her family member agrees to help provide healthy food options during the week, avoiding too much sugar and nonessential fats. She also discovers that developing an organizational structure with another member of her collaborative team prevents her from going "off track." In the past, pursuing a significant goal caused her thoughts and ideas to stack up too high, or race far ahead of her initial plan. In her post-stabilization strategy, she discusses her ideas first, with a willingness to receive feedback. With that, she can practice her interview, and with reasonable calm, see her goal to completion.

Now she's ready for her interview. And guess what? She does great! In the first ending of our example here, Sylvia gets the job.

She feels rightfully excited and proud of attaining her goal. And she celebrates her victory with her loved ones, especially anyone who helped her through the process. Now, what's next?

Knowing that life factors following goal attainment can become catalysts for mania, she takes time to explore her terrific emotions and thoughts that emanate from them. And there it is: "A new job?" she exclaims. "I need more clothes!"

During pre-stabilization, Sylvia would often go on shopping sprees while in the manic zone. Through mood-stabilizing treatment, her impulsive behaviors quelled, but she's never forgotten the thrill of acquiring various combinations of fashionable clothes for all occasions, along with several ones she never used. When the thought of buying new clothes for her new job surfaced, she was prepared. Recall one of her life values questions: "How will I manage an increased salary?"

Here is her opportunity to appreciate goal attainment while maintaining therapeutic contact with her therapist after the goal is reached. She can slow down the potential for manic recurrence through values exploration. She can also develop new, concrete responses to hold herself accountable while building on her successes in a responsible manner. In this case, she's earmarked her pay increase for a retirement account and a college fund for her child, who once suffered anxiety in response to her untreated mood swings.

If you're a bipolar patient who is in the process of reorganizing your life in post-stabilization, consider developing your own goal attainment strategy. Make sure it includes an appreciation for your own creative process, and an exploration of your personal values through specific values questions. Develop an organizational plan that includes time for proper nutrition, exercise, and, most importantly, quality sleep. Then discuss your strategy with your therapist. Explore how to mix hard work and dedication with patience in the new creative process. Also make sure to openly investigate any lack of inspiration or feelings of dullness, knowing that all of us can slog through problems at times in life. Finally, when you reach your goal, enjoy and be happy, but remain vigilant for manic recurrences that can follow goal attainment. Review your values questions at that point, especially with your therapist, so you can build on your successes while keeping manic symptoms in check.

Managing Negative Life Events

For people managing bipolar disorder in the post-stabilization phase, difficult life events—especially those that occur outside of one's control—can create risk for a recurrence of bipolar depression. We've learned that mania is a defense against depression, but with much of the manic symptoms controlled through treatment, depression can surface without defense through negative situations and the emotions they produce.

Bipolar patients typically have some perceived control over goal attainment that has the potential for manic recurrence. Manic relapse prevention focuses on how they manage goal attainment within what they can control in their lives, such as developing an organizational plan, keeping a balanced schedule, and practicing a skill for better results. But stressful, negative life events that they do not have perceived control over can result in a depressive recurrence. Thus, focusing on better management of negative life events can prevent a depression in the post-stabilization phase.

Improved life event management concentrates first on the person's perceived level of control of the negative event. It's important to assess your level of control in these situations. Some events are completely outside of your control. Some are not. And some events are partly outside of your control, but with a measure of opportunity for you to affect the outcome. Going through a negative life event can be confusing, especially when trying to figure out the cause. We can sometimes wrongly blame ourselves for things we could've never controlled. And sometimes, we avoid looking at anything we could have done better that could have reduced the event's impact.

Negative life events can involve so many different things, including grief over personal losses in relationships, money, social connections, health, career, or broken dreams of success and happiness. For young people, social losses can be especially hard to overcome. Unexpected changes in life that create fear and uncertainty will always put mood stability to the test.

Therapy is a good place to sort out all negative life-event factors. Discussing the event with a therapist offers the chance to release emotions and understand the causes to assess what can be actually done about it. Good mental health begins with understanding the difference between the things we can control and the things we can't, and having the courage to take the right course of action. It's a simple formula, but of course, living it day-to-day can be emotionally challenging.

In our example of Sylvia taking on the goal attainment of a new job, the first ending of the story finds her winning the job and then preventing a manic recurrence following the successful outcome. Now let's take a look at the alternative ending to this example. In this scenario, Sylvia doesn't get the job, despite all her best efforts toward goal attainment, both in preparation and performance. She is saddened, confused, and even somewhat angry at the loss. And not just because she didn't get the job. She's also discouraged with her new "non-manic" approach to goal attainment. She may ask herself, "If moderation and homeostasis are supposed to be so effective, how come I didn't win? Should I have avoided the approach, and stayed up all night to prepare? Should I have stayed off bipolar medication for the week?" Or perhaps she gets down on herself for having bipolar disorder in the first place: "Maybe I'm just a mentally ill freak who's not meant to succeed in life."

These doubts are common following an important negative life event in post-stabilization, especially following a new, more balanced approach. Disappointment in the process is likely. However, there also can be feelings of inappropriate guilt; she may believe she should have controlled factors that were actually outside of her control, including how the final hiring decision was made.

At this point, Sylvia is at risk for major depression. Because denial associated with mania was not present in the approach, she cannot immediately fall back on grandiosity to rationalize the loss. She cannot just convince herself in a manic style, "Hey, I'm great and they have no idea what they're missing!" Instead, she must face a "defeat" in her life—one that may be truly unfair to her, as well as outside of her ultimate control.

This is also a good time to consult her therapist. Discussing the depth of her disappointment and self-doubt can relieve her of immediate tension, and work through grief from this particular loss. Only then can an exploration of what she did well in the process and what else she could have done better can be outlined. This type of therapeutic conversation seeks to balance what can't be controlled and what can be controlled (i.e., improved in process and performance without feelings of guilt), so there can be better outcomes in the future.

I have found that successful bipolar therapy will always include an exploration of the patient's lifelong struggles with failure and success. I believe that achieving meaningful achievements in life often follow experiences of failure. Certainly, any sense of failure can threaten your self-esteem and cause you to question who you are and what you're doing. But if you generally look at your failures as opportunities to learn, and avoid depression in spite of those negative events, you will discover your eventual achievements. Because of certain conflicts from childhood, not all of us absorb failure in a healthy fashion, or for that matter, know how to accept success in a proper context. And with previously untreated bipolar mood swings, sorting out what success and failure can mean in the big picture of life is even more challenging.

With good follow-up care, Sylvia avoids falling into the major depression zone. She eventually recovers from her loss, determining that the sense of defeat is temporary, and that other opportunities will become available to her. And she will be better prepared for them next time because she's made positive efforts to manage this negative life event.

Some life events can be very tragic and completely outside of your control. The more severe the event, the more at risk a bipolar patient can be, even in post-stabilization. Extra attention is required with traumatic events, such as an unexpected death of a loved one, or a devastating loss in health, relationships, or personal security. In these circumstances, there's no waiting around. Immediate treatment is needed to avoid a severe relapse of any bipolar symptoms.

In any circumstance during post-stabilization, if manic or depressive symptoms are resurfacing, it's important to visit the prescribing physician as soon as possible. Changing meds or their dosages can be very helpful in reducing mania in goal attainment and depression in negative life events. With the assistance of medication adjustments, people with bipolar can get back to a healthy, positive post-stabilization experience.

Notes

1. Centers for Disease Control (2017, March 2). How much sleep do I need? Retrieved June 30, 2017, from https://www.cdc.gov/sleep/about_sleep/how_much_sleep.html
2. Miklowitz, D. J., & Johnson, S. L. (2009). Social and familial factors in the course of bipolar disorder: Basic processes and relevant interventions. *Clinical Psychology, 16*(2), 281–296.

CHAPTER 9

• • • • • •

Postpartum Onset in Bipolar Disorder

I'S NOT UNCOMMON FOR WOMEN with a genetic predisposition for bipolar disorder to experience mood swings during pregnancy or after childbirth. For many of these women, it may be the first time that bipolar symptoms have emerged in their lives. Sometimes symptoms of mania or depression occur with a woman's first pregnancy or delivery, sometimes with a subsequent one, and sometimes with each one. In any case, bipolar disorder related to pregnancy and childbirth can have serious effects on mother, baby, and family. But just like other instances of bipolar disorder, knowing what to look for, and how to both prevent and treat bipolar disorder before and after childbirth, can save lives and improve family life.

Before you understand how childbirth can be catalytic for bipolar, let's clarify the term I'll be using. You may hear different terms within this subject, so let's first simplify things. The technical term here is *bipolar disorder, peripartum onset*. The *peri-* refers to both "during and after" and *-partum* means "birth." However, most people including many professionals generally use the term *postpartum*, which technically refers to after-childbirth only. And perhaps making it more confusing is a host of other medical terms you may hear or read about related to the subject. For our purposes, I'm using the more common term of *postpartum*; but bear in mind, we are covering symptoms that can start anywhere from early pregnancy to days or weeks following delivery.

In recent years, postpartum major depression has been increasingly discussed in the medical community. That's good news, because previously, psychiatric symptoms in new mothers have been sadly neglected. I believe that we have only recently come to understand how awful the condition can be, and how many women have suffered without adequate treatment and support. In the past, when a new mother showed signs of depression, others viewed her as flawed. Her severe sadness, social withdrawal, or despondency were thought to be a refusal of the responsibilities of motherhood, or that she hated her baby, or she was "just overly emotional because she's a woman," or any number of judgments born out of ignorance. And what's worse is that many new mothers may have believed the stigmas they heard, reinforcing the strange thoughts and feelings that come from major depression. Certainly, most new mothers can feel overwhelmed by their new role in life, and common anxieties around motherhood can play a part in the overall condition. But a complete appreciation of postpartum hormonal and brain chemistry changes has been missing in helping new mothers recover their physical and psychological well-being. With proper assessment and treatment, women can regain homeostasis while knowing the condition they've suffered is not their fault, and discovering that they are indeed good, loving, and capable mothers.

While there's greater understanding about postpartum major depression as a unique kind of mental health problem, there's less awareness about postpartum bipolar disorder. Just as bipolar disorder is frequently misidentified as major depression alone, there's similar confusion when treating postpartum women with a bipolar predisposition. This section will help you identify if you've been suffering from postpartum bipolar disorder and how to prevent the onset or recurrence of bipolar symptoms if you are or soon to be pregnant. And this information is not just important for new mothers. New fathers, family members, and anyone in a supportive role can benefit from understanding what postpartum bipolar disorder is—and what to do about it.

When Bipolar Starts Before or After Childbirth

Let's start by looking at a first-time presentation of postpartum bipolar disorder. When starting during pregnancy, bipolar symptoms of either depression or mania are largely the result of radically changing chemicals in the body associated with the pregnancy. These hormonal and brain chemical changes can be catalytic for bipolar when the woman has the genetic bipolar predisposition. But without understanding the connection to possible bipolar onset, any further inquiry about the symptoms, along with discovering the personal and family mental health histories, is often dismissed. A pregnant woman who becomes depressed may simply be thought of as having "a bad pregnancy." And a woman with hypomanic or even some manic symptoms could be looked at as having "a great pregnancy," because she may appear so upbeat and happy. Or with dysphoric mania, she might be just given space to get through irritability and agitation, as if the symptoms are only temporary. Those around her might say, "Just leave her alone until she gets over this." In any instance, the condition is often seen as a temporary part of pregnancy, and will go away once the baby arrives. However, these symptoms could be the start to a chronic mental illness that can far exceed childbirth.

Similar problems can occur when the first-time presentation of bipolar symptoms emerge following childbirth. Depressive symptoms can be easily associated with various common childbirth issues, such as physical pain and exhaustion, problems with breastfeeding, medical concerns with the newborn, and personal and family anxieties around a major life adjustment. Manic symptoms are often mistaken for the anxious excitement, over-stimulation, or intense elation due to birthing and receiving a new child. Because manic-type behaviors may be previously un-characteristic of the woman, they are often attributed to the extraordinary event of childbirth, not internal causes. Depressive and manic-appearing symptoms are often expected to resolve as life settles down and all early concerns, fears, and excitement abate. But when a woman has a genetic predisposition to bipolar disorder, these are very likely signs that bipolar disorder has ar-rived right along with her baby.

Noticeable bipolar symptoms may not be so immediate—they may occur in the days or weeks following delivery. Sometimes the symptoms of untreated postpartum major depression can persist for a long time, producing several potentially dangerous conse-quences, including suicidal thoughts or actions. Some women with underlying bipolar disorder may stay in a depressive mood zone for an indefinite period. But sometimes the symptoms can develop slowly and shift variably. Imagine a new mother without any bipolar treatment starting with postpartum depression symp-toms, but then improving, allowing her to move into the baseline zone. She would probably decide that her depressive symptoms were only temporary, a part of her adjustment to motherhood, and that idea may be reinforced by others around her. Whatever severe personal doubts she felt about her ability to care for her new baby have retreated, and she feels fine. But lo and behold, she later swings into a manic zone. Suddenly, she not only be-lieves that she has personally overcome the "post-baby blues," she has evolved into... Super Mom!

And there is no stopping her—at least not right away. Any or all of the manic symptoms discussed earlier in this book can take hold of her in the postpartum onset. And they are often expressed in the context of her new Super Mom identity. She may find her-self rushing around town, buying all the best baby clothes. She may sign up for all available new mother activities, stay up all night cleaning and purifying the house or downloading preschool applications, because her accelerated mind insists that you can't start these things too soon! But as we've come to understand, there is a "wall" that a person in a manic zone will hit. The crash for a woman with postpartum bipolar is a painful and lonely one.

While still in mania, her euphoric energy and expanded identity can turn quickly dysphoric. She may feel thwarted or misunderstood by others, and act out in hostility against them. A frequent target for agitation is the new father or significant other involved in raising the child. An otherwise natural sense of maternal protection following childbirth might intensify beyond reality in a manic zone, creating suspicion and anger against family, friends, and neighbors. Then, after the manic zone ends, she may dive further back into depression, feeling like a failure as a mother, wife, and friend. At this point, it's not unusual at all for a new mother to wonder if her baby would be better off without her, or should have never been born in the first place.

In some cases, postpartum mania or depression can reach all the way to the psychotic zones. This is where the risks to mother and baby are the greatest. The mother may hear "voices" telling her to harm herself or the baby. Or that the baby was born of the devil, or any number of bizarre and disturbing ideas about who she or the baby have become. She may develop delusions or paranoia, losing the ability to comprehend that her out-of-control moods—not her own typical beliefs and values—are driving these unreal thoughts.

Treating the Postpartum Woman

The bottom line is that treatment for postpartum onset bipolar disorder is absolutely necessary. But just like other occurrences of bipolar, it can often go unidentified, mistreated, or completely untreated. When mood disturbances are recognized, they are often misdiagnosed as major depression. And by now, you probably can guess some of the typical treatment problems from misidentified mood swings. The big one is treating bipolar mood swings with antidepressant medications alone. While for many women antidepressants can certainly improve postpartum major depression, for women with bipolar, they can be catalytic for mania. And since dysphoric mania can be confused with depression, bipolar patients exclusively on antidepressants can see their bipolar disorder get worse. When the bipolar symptoms that are thought to be major depression don't appear to be improving, greater doses of antidepressants are sometimes prescribed, which can create very complicated, long-term problems.

However, there are also some particular issues in postpartum bipolar disorder. We have discussed how denial and fear can interfere with seeking bipolar treatment in general. Many new mothers can also live in denial and fear, but have very specific concerns with how others will perceive their postpartum bipolar symptoms. Women who experience postpartum mood swings can ask themselves, "If I tell people about my crazy thoughts and feelings, will they see me as an unfit mother? Will I go to jail? Will they take my baby away?" Mothers with postpartum bipolar disorder can carry lots of fear and shame, and avoid disclosure of their symptoms, leaving themselves feeling isolated and alone. And there may be times when these fears are based in some reality.

Think of a new mother who may be in a very contentious relationship, maybe even embroiled in a divorce proceeding. Or perhaps she's in some kind of legal trouble. Or is dependent on family members who do not accept the reality of mental illness. These situations can intensify fears about losing her child. Confused and vulnerable, it's understandable why she may not want to reach out for help. But reaching out to the right professionals and other trusted individuals can begin a treatment process that will strive to protect the mother and baby.

Much of the ambiguity associated with postpartum bipolar disorder could be prevented with medical evaluations that include personal and mental health histories created when a pregnant woman first sees a physician. This could certainly take some pressure off the pregnant woman if she needs motivation to discuss her symptoms. If the woman has a history of depression and anxiety, especially if it's recurrent, or she has had manic or hypomanic symptoms already, then she certainly is at risk for postpartum bipolar disorder. But just as important, what does the family history reveal? If a relative—particularly a close one—has had bipolar disorder or some other serious mental illness, the new mother is also at significant risk of developing those symptoms. Being proactive in understanding mental health histories means being fully prepared, just as new mothers do their best at taking care of their physical health. Since first-time symptoms may emerge while the mother is under the care of an obstetrician or other prenatal specialist, those providers could be the first contact for mental health care. Thankfully, more obstetricians, gynecologists, and various reproductive health providers are interested in postpartum mental health problems, and can initiate the treatment process when mood disorders arise.

But as we know, bipolar disorder can be far more complicated, and the patient may not bring these issues up when visiting the doctor. Patients and families need to understand what these symptoms are and how to identify them. If you or someone you love is experiencing postpartum bipolar symptoms for the first time, the first thing to understand is that these strange thoughts and feelings are nobody's fault and do not reflect the real person inside. They are the result of a genetically based brain condition that was triggered by hormonal changes. And because of this, it's absolutely necessary to inform the doctor about it right away. Early intervention is the best path to success. If you're a new mother, it's understandable why you might be scared to ask questions and leave yourself open to negative judgments or worse. And that's especially true if you had thoughts of harming yourself or your baby due to the severe effects of postpartum bipolar disorder.

Let's look at some positive ways to talk with your doctor, even if the physician is not a mental health specialist. If you suspect you have postpartum bipolar disorder, but don't want to reveal every detail right away, you can ask questions in a general sequence until you get answers that inspire more confidence that help is available and without risk to you. It may also be best to have a supportive individual in the meeting with you, if possible.

Here are some questions to ask your doctor:

- Are you familiar with postpartum mood disorders?
- How often do you see postpartum mood disorders in your patients?
- Do you treat those disorders?
- If so, what's your approach to treatment?
- If not, who do you refer to for postpartum treatment?
- Are you specifically familiar with postpartum bipolar disorder?
- How do you approach (or your recommended doctor approaches) bipolar mood swings?
- What's your opinion about medications during pregnancy?
- What's your opinion about medications during breastfeeding?

If the doctor can answer these questions in a way that gives you both sound information and a greater sense of hope, then you can provide more details if needed. If the doctor provides a referral, contact the recommended doctor as soon as possible. If this is the start of bipolar disorder, you will eventually need to seek mental health professionals familiar with bipolar anyway, because you'll be facing all the typical bipolar therapy issues through post-stabilization. But some early peace of mind that help is within reach is your best place to start. The objectives here include gaining a positive sense of hope for yourself, the ability to care for yourself, and moving from pre-stabilization through stabilization as efficiently as possible.

Notice I didn't say anything about being the best *mom* you can be. If you're suffering from postpartum bipolar disorder, winning the gold medal for Mother of the Year is not the priority right now. If you don't take care of yourself and get involved in treatment as soon as you can, you'll struggle to care for your baby, your family, and all other adult responsibilities. And that will be true no matter what grandiose ideas you have about yourself when in a manic zone. Good bipolar treatment means you'll eventually be in the best position to bond with your child, and develop a calmer, more consistent demeanor that will build good mental health for both of you. This is the essence of being a good mother—not just what you do for the child, but who you are in the presence of that child. And proper bipolar care allows you to be your best self.

If you're the loved one of the mother with postpartum bipolar, know that you'll be needed to care for the baby and support the mother as she moves through the stabilization phase of bipolar therapy. It's very difficult for new fathers and other supportive family members to face postpartum bipolar amid the flurry of activity around a new baby. The pressures to keep up a job, finances, household chores, and perhaps the needs of other children at home are difficult enough, let alone having this overwhelming problem of postpartum bipolar thrown into the mix. And, for that matter, the new mother may not be as "radiant" as you'd like her to be. Instead, she can be intensely sad, anxious, agitated, or simply unreasonable to deal with. Know that through stabilization, you will have your opportunity to work through your feelings and highlight your needs to create a more stable existence for the whole family. The first priority is to get to stabilization as efficiently as possible, and you are instrumental in that pursuit. And while denial may be present as you attempt to confront the bipolar problem, I have found that many women appreciate knowing that their mood condition has a name and a treatment. Her knowledge that you don't blame her for mood swings, especially when she is agitated, gives you an advantage in providing loving support going forward.

Many of the same general bipolar therapy issues in the pre-stabilization and stabilization phases apply in postpartum bipolar disorder. But the big question that postpartum bipolar patients will ask is "How will taking medications affect my baby?" This is especially concerning when the bipolar onset is during pregnancy but also an issue with respect to breastfeeding. We've already explored this medication issue previously, but I believe it bears some revisiting. That's because when discussing medications with your prescribing physician, it's important to remember that untreated bipolar mood swings can have negative effects on fetal development (while the baby is in the uterus) and emotional attachment between the mother and baby after delivery.

As I have mentioned, deciding on bipolar medications during pregnancy is a personal decision that can come from frank discussions with your doctor and family. But you should not consider all meds bad for fetal health. For example, the mood stabilizers lamotrigine and lithium can offer reasonable treatment options during pregnancy.[1] On the other hand, untreated mood disorders can actually reduce fetal growth and affect certain aspects of the baby's neurological development.[2] During pregnancy you must weigh the pros and cons of bipolar meds, knowing that active bipolar symptoms may ultimately have far more detriment to the baby's health.

After birth, med-related issues center around breastfeeding (lactation) and the need for maternal-child emotional attachment, or bonding. Certainly, breastfeeding has terrific nutritional and psychological advantages. And it can be an effective means for the mother and child to "get to know each other" in a very basic and beautiful way. However, if bipolar symptoms are active and untreated, depression and mania can impair the bonding process profoundly. Whatever benefits that come from breastfeeding could be seriously offset by the mother's mood swings. Consider the new baby's first emotional experiences of intense disconnections during mom's depression, and the intense overactivity and agitation during her mania. Infants benefit from feeling a sense of predictability and consistency in how their physical and emotional needs are handled. This gives them a sense of safety in the world around them. When emotional messages to the baby are unpredictable and chaotic, it's much harder to feel safe. And these messages can be embedded in a baby's mind as he or she develops into early childhood.

Nothing in life is perfectly predictable, and even infants can be somewhat resilient to change around them. But in assessing whether to take medications while breastfeeding or stop breast-feeding to take medications, it's good to weigh the pros and cons, as well. If the goal is to have a rich and meaningful bonding experience, mood stability is front and center in that effort. If you're a new mother struggling with bipolar and are somewhat late to the treatment process, you may be worried that you've screwed up your baby for life. But you needn't worry about that. It's not too late to get help. Through bipolar therapy, you'll have plenty of opportunity to help your child feel safe and happy through the stabilization process.

And for all new mothers who've experienced postpartum bipolar disorder, life gets better through post-stabilization. Remember that bipolar disorder is a lifelong condition, no matter the age or circumstances of onset. It won't just go away once the baby is born. But with the right care and support, it doesn't have to define the mother or her parenting. It can result in many more days in a baseline mood zone, which offers her a positive motherhood experience.

Notes

1. Grover, S., & Avasthi, A. (2015). Mood stabilizers in pregnancy and lactation. *Indian Journal of Psychiatry, 57*(Suppl 2), S308-23.
2. Kingston, D., Tough, S., & Whitfield, H. (2012). Prenatal and postpartum maternal psychological distress and infant development: A systematic review. *Child Psychiatry & Human Development, 43*(5), 683–714.

CHAPTER 10

• • • • • • •

Hospital/Inpatient Treatment

MOST TREATMENT FOR BIPOLAR DISORDER can be performed in an outpatient setting (mainly the therapist's or doctor's office), but in many instances, inpatient treatment is needed. That's because severe episodes of mania or depression can have immediate life-threatening consequences. Even if you believe a hospital admission for bipolar disorder is unlikely, it's good to prepare yourself for it. Because knowledge is power, you can better understand what to expect when hospitalization becomes necessary to own bipolar disorder under particular circumstances.

Modern Inpatient Treatment

Modern inpatient mental health treatment doesn't resemble the frightening images and arcane approaches that characterized institutions of old. Lacking the array of treatment options available today, the hospitals and asylums of yesteryear would often either keep patients for extremely long stays, or employ radical or experimental treatments that could result in a host of medical and psychological consequences. These days, hospital treatments are far better, more effective, and require shorter stays than before. Patients are treated with compassion and provided activities to improve their mental and social functioning. Even with the most serious of psychiatric cases, the goal is to move each patient out of the hospital and into community-based treatments as soon as clinically acceptable.

Despite the improvements in inpatient care, however, no hospital has had every treatment go exactly as planned because humans run institutions. And as we've learned, bipolar disorder can be difficult to treat. It's essential to maintain a clear and balanced mind-set when inpatient treatment is needed. We must trust the inpatient process but also develop a means to communicate and keep up with what's going on while stabilization is progressing. We should avoid trusting without being actively involved in the process or becoming too skeptical before allowing the treatment team to do its job. For family members, acting as supportive collaborators with hospital staff members can minimize disruptions to a positive outcome.

For those with severe levels of bipolar symptoms, including those from psychotic mania or psychotic depression, inpatient treatment often is necessary to achieve at least the initial goal toward stabilization—symptom reduction. The level of agitation and potential for self-harm must be quickly evaluated and medicated. No hospital would allow a new manic patient to endanger self, staff members, or other patients. The high levels of mania and psychotic symptoms have to be reduced as much as possible. A hospital is usually the best place to achieve this. Around-the-clock monitoring by a professional staff can ensure safety for the patient and maintain the integrity of the hospital environment.

Stabilization in a hospital setting takes a different approach compared with an outpatient setting. When bipolar patients—especially manic ones—are admitted, they usually present pronounced symptoms requiring intensive medical intervention.

Medications could be quite sedating, which might be the treatment pattern for several hours to several days before the patient becomes balanced, coherent, and reasonable to a certain degree.

It can be shocking for family members to see their bipolar loved one on high doses of mood-stabilizing or antipsychotic medications. Patients with these immediate treatment needs won't be "back to normal" right away; they might be tranquilized and dazed for a time. Even after the crisis has settled down, they could remain psychotic and delusional to some extent. The sedation aspect tends to be more rapidly achieved than full relief from manic or depressive symptoms. If the bipolar patient has been abusing alcohol or other drugs, a medical detoxification process may be needed before the patient can be treated from the psychiatric perspective. This process can take hours to days to ensure the patient is safe from the effects of substances. This is important from a withdrawal standpoint, but crucial if an overdose is suspected.

If the hospital is a full medical/surgical facility with a psychiatric unit, the detox could be done on site. But most inpatient psychiatric hospitals are stand-alone facilities that only treat psych disorders, and some won't have detox capability. In that case, patients would be immediately referred or transported to a hospital that can provide detox services, after which they can return for specific bipolar treatment.

This obviously can be a tense period for the patient and family. Hospitalization could have several origins: a request by an outpatient doctor or therapist due to an extreme pre-stabilization crisis, the result of a 911 call from a family member or neighbor, or a self-generated call while under extreme duress. Also, law enforcement can initiate the admission involuntarily by suspecting the patient was in imminent danger to self or others. Therefore, inpatient care is weighed toward an emergency approach. That means the treatment plan is designed to quickly defuse the crisis and reduce the high level of symptoms that accompany it.

It can be scary to watch a bipolar loved one taken through the large doors of a psychiatric unit, leaving you wondering what will happen next. Family members need to be kept apprised of the immediate procedures involved and the course of treatment planned. If they're left wondering, then fears surrounding hospital treatment will fill the void of knowledge. And when fear takes over, anger often arises.

Working with the Hospital Staff

In the early phase of stabilization, family members can turn against hospital staff members or each other, especially if they're unfamiliar with the facility or the treatment course under such extreme situations. You can imagine how often hospital staff members witness the patient's immediate crises as well as frenzied responses from family members. Hospital employees are responsible for maintaining a calm, safe environment, and they're usually trained to reduce fear and tensions among family members at this critical juncture. But hospitals—whether large urban facilities or smaller rural centers—are human institutions with busy routines and competing demands.

When a bipolar loved one is being admitted for inpatient treatment, it's a good time to get to know a staff member on-site and form a collaborative relationship. This ideally should occur at the initial evaluation for admission, often known as the "intake."

The intake counselor discusses the situation completely and explains the hospital program. But that shouldn't be the last contact. During regular business hours, there almost always is someone to talk to, but after hours, available staff is likely limited. Nonetheless, the front desk can pass along important messages, including requests to speak with the on-duty nurse.

If your loved one has bipolar disorder and staff members don't know it, it's absolutely necessary to inform them. If you're speaking with a nontreatment staff member, find out who the attending doctor or nurse is. You could say, "I'd like to make sure they know my husband has bipolar disorder. Whom can I speak to about it?"

If you're told no one is available, you can reply, "I understand you're quite busy right now. Please tell me how I can be certain the nurse or doctor knows he has bipolar disorder." Your request will likely be met with some assurance, but even more likely, someone relevant to the treatment process will speak with you.

Hospital staff members appreciate family members who politely introduce themselves, provide background information on the patient, and express overall support for the staff's work. Most facilities use case managers assigned to each patient at admission, or at least by the first business day if the admission occurred on a weekend or holiday. The case managers are part of the clinical staff including social workers and other therapists. They are usually employed by the hospital to work in-house and are typically available and knowledgeable about the patient's overall care. The attending physician, if not on-site, can be contacted through the attending nurses when necessary. Face-to-face consultations are great, but phone conversations are easier for busy staff members than in person. Ultimately, they're just as effective when you have questions and concerns prepared ahead of time. (You'll probably get a patient identification number to use when you call.)

Remember, confidentiality is important in a hospital, so don't expect staff members to volunteer information without written consent from the patient and confidence that you're a trusted individual in the patient's care. That's true even if you're the patient's spouse, adult child, or sibling.

Attitude of Collaboration

Many family members, even with sincere intentions, try to interfere with treatment. But you're different because you're collaborating with the treatment team.

An inpatient admission for bipolar disorder should never be handled like dry cleaning—just drop it off and pick it up when it's clean and wrinkle-free. Treatment staff members need your factual support, and your loved one needs your moral support. That is too important to neglect, even if you're exhausted and angry.

This also isn't the time for major life changes. There can be exceptions in extreme cases, such as in relationships with physical abuse, but if major life decisions can be delayed, then do so. That gives the emergency treatment its best chance to help the patient stabilize. (You'll see opportunities to address relationship issues as the stabilization phase completes in Chapter 11.)

Inquire about standard family services the treatment program might provide. This includes therapy or educational groups onsite or near the hospital. Avail yourself of any support available to you. You will be a better team member during the treatment process if you are taken care of too.

Group Therapy Opportunities

Most hospital patients attend group therapy sessions staffed by professional counselors or psychotherapists. The bulk of inpatient therapy occurs in these groups, which are a key component of the emergency stabilization process. Most programs allow patients to rest as they overcome the sedative aspect of medications, but they'll eventually be roused from their rooms and encouraged to attend the groups.

If you're a patient, you may or may not enjoy the opportunity to speak your mind freely among strangers. Many manic patients enjoy the attention they receive in group therapy but depressed patients often prefer to be left alone. To the group therapist, it doesn't matter. The point is to begin immediate group contact and discussions with others facilitated by the therapist. Occupational, recreational, and creative therapies offer opportunities for personal growth and a complete treatment experience.

In conducting group therapy in inpatient settings, I've found the sooner patients join that process the sooner they feel a part of a therapeutic community. Group therapy gives patients a chance to share their stories, emotional pain, and relationship conflicts in a place of safety and acceptance. It reduces shame and fear while bonding people who seek mutual recovery goals. Hearing the stories of others and sharing information about medications and treatment outcomes can inspire questions and new ideas. Some patients resist attending groups at first, mostly due to the fight-or-flight response. When faced with uncertain circumstances amid strangers, it's natural to look for differences in others as a matter of defense.

If you are attending group therapy—especially in a hospital setting—I encourage you to discover commonalities between yourself and other participants despite outward differences. You might form bonds you never knew were possible. As scary as it may seem at first, group therapy allows you to connect with people who intimately understand what it's like to struggle with mental illness. In adult and adolescent inpatient programs where I've worked, many patients who loudly resisted treatment when they were admitted just as loudly resisted discharge when it was time to go home!

Achieving Treatment Goals

Nonetheless, "When can I go home" is one of the first questions patients ask at the start of inpatient care. The answer usually depends on achieving these requirements:

- Adequate reduction of bipolar symptoms
- Assured safety for the patient and those in the patient's life
- A solid aftercare plan

Remember that the doctors and therapists who are treating you during a hospital stay might not be the same providers after discharge. If there's an outpatient treatment team before admission, the hospital team should be apprised of all treatment

activity so there can be continuity of care during and after the inpatient stay. Make sure the transition back to the outpatient
providers goes smoothly.

If you don't have a doctor or therapist before hospitalization,
don't assume the in-house doctors or therapists will provide treatment afterward. If you like your treating doctor, ask if he or she is
available for office visits. If not, or if you'd prefer working with
someone else, get all the proper referrals to set up appointments
before discharge. Patient perceptions of collaboration, empathy,
and availability of their treatment providers increases adherence
to their continuing care.[1] You need a solid aftercare plan to continue your journey from stabilization to post-stabilization. Without
it, the chance of returning to a pre-stabilization crisis is high.

A good aftercare plan usually is formed with the guidance of
the hospital case manager. You can make appointments through
the case manager or on your own. Make sure to select providers
who are familiar with bipolar disorder and the special needs its
treatment requires. Outpatient treatment sessions should follow
hospital discharge as soon as possible.

If you've improved enough to leave inpatient care, but are not
yet ready for a complete transition to outpatient visits in your doctor's or therapist's office, many hospitals have partial programs.
These are often referred to as a partial hospitalization program
(PCP) or intensive outpatient program (IOP). These treatment
programs offer many of the same services during the day, but
allow you to return home in the evening. Some even offer programs after business hours, so that you can return to work.

Participating in support groups can help you continue the
process you achieved in the hospital. Inpatient programs sometimes offer aftercare groups for ongoing connection, so ask what
the program has to offer. If alcohol or drug dependency is an
issue, get involved in a sobriety-oriented group such as Alcoholics Anonymous.

Your living arrangements should never be taken for granted,
either. You need a solid, reliable place to live during transition

from inpatient care. For example, if a patient was living in a car before hospitalization, returning to the car threatens to undermine the good work done in the hospital. A trusted family member needs to be involved. Finding a mental health or sober-living residential facility can be essential in this transition time.

While hospitals are places we'd like to stay away from, for intensive bipolar treatment, an inpatient program can be life-saving. Owning bipolar means being open to different treatment options to meet an individual's need, including hospitalization. Collaboration with hospital staff during treatment and good aftercare planning prior to discharge can resolve a pre-stabilization crisis, while beginning a solid stabilization experience.

Notes

1. Sylvia, L. G., Hay, A., & Ostacher, M. J. (2013). Association between therapeutic alliance, care satisfaction, and pharmacological adherence in bipolar disorder. *Journal of Clinical Psychopharmacology, 33*(3), 343–350.

CHAPTER 11

Need for Support from Families and Beyond

To take full ownership of bipolar, family members should be actively involved in support and care—for the person with bipolar and for themselves. This chapter will show you common family issues, and how to be better prepared for therapy together. Evidence shows that family involvement in therapy and education greatly improves treatment outcomes.[1] That support, though, requires a reasonable selection of participants, thorough education on the disorder, and refined methods of interaction. A limited number of people should be involved in the process, and not everyone is invited. Those who are invited can learn and grow in owning bipolar together with the patient.

Family members include anyone the patient chooses such as a/an:

- Spouse
- Intimate partner
- Parent
- Parent figure

167

- Adult child
- Sibling
- Extended family member
- Friend or associate

The ideal is to engage people who you trust, have maturity and character, and are in a position to observe. The most trusted people might not be suitable because of physical distance or personal issues that prevent them from being fully involved. Spousal involvement is typically necessary, but many times the patient mistrusts the spouse—at least at the start of treatment. Parents of adolescents should be involved, but the young patient could trust one parent more than the other. This is especially common with divorced parents or when stepparents are in the picture. Friends and associates may not immediately be thought of as family, but many patients have friends they confide in and trust more than their blood relatives. And a close business associate might need to know about a colleague's bipolar disorder to improve their working relationship, especially if they're business partners.

I initiate this conversation with the patient at the start of treatment without assuming who the identified family members are or should be. A patient can exclude expected individuals, but that doesn't mean he or she doesn't love them. Those family members may become a part of bipolar treatment at some point, such as during the post-stabilization phase.

Giving patients the option of who will become part of their treatment assists in their ownership of the process. This is especially important to inspire confidentiality in one-on-one sessions.

Confidentiality is also protected by a set of legal and ethical rules about the privacy between therapist/doctor and patient. This means a doctor cannot discuss an adult patient's medical information without the specific consent of the patient. Only an adult patient (18 or older) can give consent through written release for the therapist to speak with any assigned individual about his or her treatment. Exceptions include suspected child or elder abuse, or if the patient is in imminent danger to self or others. If the patient is a minor (17 or younger), then only a parent or guardian can provide written consent. However, differing state laws permit underage children to acquire therapy services without parental consent, especially if safety issues are suspected.

Because of this right to confidentiality, I don't demand that a patient give consent to having a family member involved. However, I discuss how this involvement can improve treatment outcomes and lead to a happier family life. Even with their consent, I don't always discuss every aspect of individual treatment with the family member(s) involved. I make sure the patient knows ahead of time what to expect, and we go over methods of interaction to ensure positive results.

Involving two or three family members is helpful in successful chronic disease management.[2] Certainly one family member is better than none, but having two or three involved develops a system of supporting and checking the patient's treatment goals while reducing the burden borne by each one individually.

So why wouldn't having four or more supporters be even better? It seems too many cooks spoil the broth. In some instances, certain family members express widely differing viewpoints, which confuses the patient on what needs to be done in treatment. With too many opinions in the mix, the patient often drifts away from treatment rather than stay with a single, identifiable plan. And too many involved at the same time increases the risk of total family burnout. With two or three family members, the patient can better focus on goals without the risk of getting pulled in conflicting directions.

What is the top priority when identifying and limiting trusted family members? Keeping the patient connected through the three phases of bipolar therapy. But remember that family members have also suffered the consequences of bipolar disorder. Many need therapy, too. If you are one of them, know that your pain and fears must be taken into account. You'll need to set aside your own time to release your anger and grief, and not just be a stoic "Rock of Gibraltar" for your bipolar loved one.

Being part of bipolar care can be difficult when you've been a victim of those consequences. You may not always want to join in the process out of hurt and anger. You could be tempted to say, "He can get his own therapy and fix himself." As humans, when we feel hurt, we often look for something or someone to blame. Projecting blame is a form of denial. On the other hand, family members often complain their bipolar loved ones are moving ahead in the bipolar disorder treatment process without family members understanding what's going on or hearing any acknowledgment of what they've been through. If you're a family member feeling left out or behind in your loved one's bipolar treatment, make the effort to get caught up with the process through information and support.

Luke's Story

Luke's wife is having difficulty dealing with his bipolar diagnosis. Luke is surprised to discover that, with his life falling apart, his doctor concludes he suffers from Bipolar II. This diagnosis gives him pause to review the behaviors that have alienated him from his wife.

> My mind is always racing. I'm constantly thinking about what I have to do next. I'm a computer programmer and that keeps me busy during the day. But I don't want to come home at night; I don't know what I'm going to be blamed for next. My kids mean the world to me, and because of them I push myself to go home. My wife is always angry with me, and I get it. I did a lot of awful things and caused a lot of damage. Being diagnosed with bipolar disorder helped me understand why I did all of those things,

but it didn't seem to help my wife. She thinks I've just made bad choices. I don't know what to do so I'm just giving her time. Hopefully she'll understand some-day and forgive me, and we can move forward.

I'm going to therapy and I'm working hard at it. I want to fix things with my wife. But who knows what will happen. My kids are what makes me keep going.[3]

Audrey's Story

On the other side of the bipolar relationship equation, Audrey laments her struggle with a bipolar husband and how she has felt left out of the process.

> Everyone worries about the person with bipolar disorder, but what about the people who live with them? I know my husband needs help, and I am so grateful that he's finally getting it. But what about me? He seems to be getting to a place where he can manage his moods and emotions, but he caused so much damage and I was the one who always had to come in behind him and try to fix things. I'm tired and I'm frustrated and I want someone to recognize all that I've gone through and help me. Maybe that sounds selfish, but it's just the way I feel.[4]

Audrey speaks for so many facing bipolar in their loved ones. Without knowledge and support with bipolar as it affects her, she feels isolated and alone. Understanding how to own bipolar as a family member empowers you to recognize the "red flags" and address bipolar issues before the disease gets worse.

Bipolar disorder is not an excuse; it's an explanation. And al-though bipolar disorder is nobody's fault, treating and managing the illness is a responsibility—first of the patient, second of the family. It must occur in this order, because family members can't be expected to work harder on owning the disorder than the patient does.

If you weren't invited to participate in treatment, you still can benefit from the power of knowledge and understand what your bipolar loved one and other family members are going through. Additional family members frequently attend my education groups and gain understanding of bipolar disorder, which helps get everyone on the same track. You *can* own the bipolar disorder that pertains to your life, and you'll likely have the opportunity to get involved at the right time.

The family educational sessions I conduct teach me a lot about what's most important for people struggling with bipolar. The following points generate the most interest among participants:

- Bipolar is a genetic disorder that is no one's fault.
- It can drive impulsivity, substance abuse, and irresponsible and destructive acts.
- It can make a good, moral person do very bad things.
- It's a disease that can hide and then return without warning.
- It can ruin trust and relationships.
- It occurs, but it's not because of a lack of willpower or the absence of love.

Hearing these truths about bipolar in an educational forum helps people feel validated. They often express how relieved they are knowing they're not alone in their experiences, and they don't have to blame themselves or each other. And affirming that the person with bipolar may have acted poorly because of a disease, not a moral flaw, gives everyone the freedom to rebuild broken relationships.

Now, I will show you what to expect when you incorporate your special relationships into your bipolar treatment. Once you've read through this section, feel free to pass it on to your loved one, and discuss it together. And even if these relationships don't apply to you, I recommend reading further anyway. You will learn more about yourself and your unique relationship through what others have endured.

Spouses or Intimate Partners

Spouses and intimate partners of people with bipolar often come to the early stage of treatment in great despair. They feel alone and disregarded in the process. They've been the ones who stayed up nights wondering where their manic spouse was or worrying about their future. They have suffered with their partner during depressive episodes and saw their bank accounts dwindle during manic episodes. They have gone through a variety of emotions, including embarrassment, rejection, betrayal, and abandonment. Some even feel guilty, though they've done nothing wrong. They wonder if they didn't love or protect their spouse enough or said something wrong in a fit of anger that set things off. And they may have felt so angry and helpless, they became depressed themselves.

I usually meet the spouse in couples therapy or after the patient's initial individual sessions. In either case, spouses usually are focused on the functional consequences of bipolar and the loss of trust. Typical issues for spouses include:

- Substance abuse
- Financial losses
- Infidelity
- Verbal outbursts
- Emotional abuse
- Violence (threats or actual)
- Impulsive acts of all kinds
- Abdication of adult responsibilities

When spouses and intimate partners attend educational sessions, they appreciate hearing information about the disorder. But in therapy sessions, they want to know their pain is recognized, and they often want to make a point about their feelings. This makes sense when you think about how frequently mania dominated their interactions or how their spouse's depressive moods separated them from all interactions. And often when therapy has already started for bipolar patients, spouses may feel alone in what's happening. Maybe the patient is moving forward with therapy, medications, etc., and may be feeling and doing better in life. But the spouse may feel that he or she is expected to go along with whatever happens, and just be happy about it. If you're a spouse in this situation, you might find yourself saying, "What? Am I just supposed to think everything is great now? What about everything I went through?" As a result, you may feel "left behind" in the therapy process.

Spouses need a sense of validation about what they've lived through. This is especially true if the person with bipolar has blocked out or can't remember some manic events. Spouses need to speak openly, which will likely lead to recounting painful and embarrassing moments for either or both of them.

The purpose is not to create further shame for the bipolar patient. Rather, it's to permit the spouse to resolve pain and resentment for getting caught up with the bipolar treatment process, so they don't have to feel left behind anymore. If you're in therapy, you can't simply bury those events in the past just because bipolar treatment has begun. Every time you make progress in therapy, those memories surface in the form of anxiety and can set you back. If you're the bipolar patient, take these moments as opportunities to listen and gradually understand how bad the bipolar disorder has been for your spouse. That doesn't mean how bad *you've been*; it refers to how bad the *bipolar disorder* has been. This can reduce your feeling of shame.

In this spirit, you can certainly apologize for all the wrongdoings during your untreated mood swings and attempt to make amends, but you can only achieve real reparations through the pursuit of bipolar treatment along with your spouse.

As a spouse, you may be exhausted from all the apologies after months or years of bipolar mood swings. In therapy, most spouses are interested in how the functional consequences of bipolar mentioned earlier will be prevented. Keeping up with someone with an active bipolar disorder makes spouses wary, especially after hearing many broken promises and suffering numerous heartbreaks. As an exhausted spouse, you might finally ask the patient, "How do I know you'll never do that stuff again?"

That's a great question, but the answer is not a simple one. If you're the patient and you're not sure what else to say, "I promise that stuff will never happen again," can easily come across as glib and insincere. Real answers are provided in increments of time and achievable goals, with both patient and spouse collaborating in the bipolar treatment. When I hear this in a couple's session, I might interject with, "If you both agree to be fully involved in treatment, we can find ways to prevent going through that awful pain again."

What's the key to success here? It's for the spouse to gain access to the treatment process, so that both patient and spouse can go through the stabilization phase together, if at all possible. If you're a couple working on owning bipolar together, know that open discussions on the past effects of mood swings can bring the spouse equally into the treatment process, and increase success in the post-stabilization phase.

However, there can be different expectations through each of the three phases of bipolar therapy. A spouse doesn't always follow each phase along with the patient. The fear of re-experiencing the awful consequences of pre-stabilization can keep the spouse mentally and emotionally stuck in that phase. This happens even if the patient is going through stabilization or beyond. The spouse might want to proceed but is stopped by fear. I sometimes hear a spouse comment, "I can forgive, but I just can't forget." You might find yourself saying this privately or out loud. Either way, it's normal to feel this way. You might be afraid that "forgetting" what happened in the pre-stabilization phase is like saying to the patient in the stabilization phase, "What you did before is all okay now."

Although spouses may be behind in the treatment process initially, once they're caught up, they often want to slow it down to protect their interests. They want to ensure they won't get their hopes up sky-high, only to suffer a crash if treatment fails. They've been fooled before, and by God, they won't be fooled again!

As a result, spouses still might not be ready to move forward until all of their feelings are acknowledged with the confidence that they are truly part of the treatment plan. In this sense, they need to go through their own stabilization process. For spouses, so much of the stabilization phase is dedicated to learning forgiveness without having to forget their suffering. Ideally, it should parallel the patient's stabilization phase.

Discussing previous functional consequences of bipolar during the stabilization phase is a bold and necessary part of relationship repair. It's hard to relive those dreadful experiences. Instead, the impulse is to ignore them and press on. However, people with bipolar need to be patient with their spouses during this phase. Once the spouses gain access to treatment and feel more confident that they're a definite part of bipolar therapy, their grief and despair often turn to anger—a sign of early spousal empowerment. This is expected *and* essential to accepting the full bipolar disease!

Denial covers fear, but anger expresses it. Behind every angry display is an equally powerful fear trying to come out. For many, discussing fear reveals weakness. Anger allows for a show of strength, yet it sometimes guards deep feelings and is defensive. But in the sequence of emotions needed to achieve acceptance of bipolar, anger can be the energy that breaks through denial. As long as it doesn't seek to undermine the ultimate goal, showing anger can gain strength against the once all-powerful mania. Anger can be expressed loudly or harshly, or at times with poignant conviction. But however anger is displayed, it's best expressed in an emotionally safe environment such as the therapist's office.

Not all spouses start off treatments being sad, passive, and disoriented. Some come feeling severe anger, even rage. They might have been arguing and fighting with their bipolar loved one for a long time. As a response, anger differs from aggression and consists of a certain denial component. Aggression is the behavior that can come from the emotion of anger. And there are different levels of aggression—from passive, subtle acts that undermine trust, to acting out hostilities against each other, to the most severe form of violence. Certain couples act out aggression by yelling at each other as if they wouldn't be heard otherwise. This interpersonal style could have been learned in their families, especially if yelling in response to anger was common growing up. But add to that the power of mania and the neglect of depression in adult life, and you have a volatile brew of emotions. If these unresolved feelings have been going on for a long time, they can turn to disgust and hatred.

If the interpersonal style is to yell until heard and understood, the potential for violence increases. Violent acts can include threats or real actions causing physical or mental harm. Certainly, many people won't cross a line into violence, but domestic violence is a tragically common part of life. Ask any law enforcement officer. Pretending it will never happen to you is a form of denial.

Without a therapeutic means to resolve internal feelings of anger and ways to express it without aggression, one of two things results: aggression against the self (depression) or aggression against the other (violence).

The previously untreated bipolar patient could already have acted violently during pre-stabilization. The frightened spouse would feel better knowing that treatment could prevent future outbursts while also thinking it's unfair that his or her own deep feelings of rage must be kept under wraps. Moreover, some spouses fear that expressing their anger might incite rage in the person with bipolar, thereby complicating recovery. If this is happening to you, your needs should be directed by a trained professional who can create a therapeutic discussion that's safe and effective.

If the volume of anger is too high in your relationship or violence seems close to erupting, you may need time apart. In the early stages of relationship treatment, I sometimes meet with the patient and spouse separately to give both the opportunity to be heard. This way, I can become a container for their anger and fears—at least until the couple can safely collaborate. This approach may be necessary for you if, previously, the mania dominated your verbal exchanges with no opportunity for reason and mutual understanding to weigh in. I recommend that you consult a therapist to discuss if you're needing time apart, and how to safely have discussions to relieve that high level of anger and potential for aggression.

The stabilization phase isn't clean and neat for anyone. Treatment is typically uneven and medications may not yet be fully effective and manageable. The patient could remain in some level of denial. For the spouse, the emotional and trust consequences remain in flux. But if either spouse or patient has been holding back emotions, then letting them out in a moment of anger can be healthy and progressive. But releasing anger could cause the other to feel he or she will never move on from the ugly occurrences of bipolar.

During ther stabilization phase, the patient could say to the spouse, "You're just angry at me all the time now. You won't let go of the past and just move on." The spouse may reply, "I've been angry with you for a long time. It's just that now you're in treatment, I feel like maybe you can hear me."

From there, measured releases of anger can reduce fear and move toward forgiveness, and can promote a desire in both the patient and spouse to move forward with their lives. As a bipolar therapist, I see a great opportunity in this condition to negotiate through problems. Every successful relationship requires negotiation, give and take, and compromise. No one likes to give away anything at first; they fear loss before they anticipate gain. We learned that early in our childhoods. But as mature adults, we come to understand that compromise—giving up something to get greater returns—is essential in all interpersonal contacts.

In the stabilization phase, spouses ideally work together toward stabilization. They come to own bipolar *together*. The patient commits to maintaining treatment until the meds are manageable and the spouse agrees to process anger toward forgiveness. This isn't a simple tit-for-tat exchange or a fifty-fifty split as if they pledge, "I'll do my part *only* if you do yours." Rather, it's a serious undertaking by each one to work 100 percent toward mutual goals. Always remember that for your own relationship success, the agreement is "We can do our parts together at the same time."

To collaboratively move toward bipolar acceptance and post-stabilization, patient and spouse agree to focus on their individual efforts while supporting the other to complete the objectives. For spouses and intimate partners, the post-stabilization phase can offer both relief and cause for celebration. Pain in the early phases is replaced with hope and initial successes, while setting the stage for an intimate relationship and long-term success.

In this phase, the couple has to create a new identity for daily functioning. During the pre-stabilization phase, there was likely a "parent-child" type of relationship between them. Bipolar often forces spouses to care for many or all the adult obligations of daily life. They look forward to developing an "adult-adult" relationship that likely never existed before.

When working on a new relationship together through bipolar therapy, it's necessary to strive toward balance and reciprocity. This means giving and taking in a mutually agreeable manner that's not always at the exact same time, but feels as if there are two adults giving and receiving together to attain mutual life goals.

Before post-stabilization, bipolar created an on-again, off-again love affair complete with a push-pull in communication and intimacy. When manic, perhaps the patient was hypersexual—always ready to rock and roll. When depressed, though, that same individual was cold and withdrawn. In any instance, the bipolar patient could demonstrate any combination of emotions and desires as a surprise to an unprepared spouse.

A more moderate expression of mood and desires than before is expected in the post-stabilization phase. Both patient and spouse can better predict the condition of their relationship and how they feel about each other. However, just as patients struggle to understand if their emotions actually reflect their true selves, spouses frequently wonder, "Is it you or is it bipolar?" That question suggests every spouse needs more time and opportunity to discover the bipolar loved one's true self.

It may take time, but remember it's a process. Think of the passage of time during the post-stabilization phase as a time to create mental distance from the terrible consequences during pre-stabilization. Don't confuse this with a failure to let go of the past. Patients should understand that when they're asked, "Is it you or bipolar?" it's about discovering reality in the present. You can help your spouse understand his or her own self-discoveries by sharing new attitudes and approaches to daily life. Keep your spouse updated with the progress of your individual treatments, including changes in medications, and the struggles and breakthroughs of psychotherapy. Talk through difficult emotions you may be experiencing and discuss how you can both handle stress. This allows your spouse to be better equipped to sift the "you" from the bipolar disorder.

Parents, Stepparents, and Guardians

Parents often come to treatment with their bipolar children in various states of desperation and denial. When in denial, parents often do not think there's anything wrong and attribute bipolar-related consequences to adolescence gone haywire. If you're a parent or in a parent role, it's important to have the right education and support as you come to accept bipolar disorder in your child, while also facing all the challenges of your child growing up.

Bipolar disorder is a mental illness of mostly young people; the average age of Bipolar I onset is 18. Identifying the disorder in adolescence (or earlier if possible) is one of the greatest gifts that those children could receive. I know people—parents and professionals alike—can be afraid to attach the bipolar label to a young person. It's as if they fear the diagnosis more than the disease. Or they believe their child has bipolar but are afraid the label will follow them for life.

Despite strict rules governing confidentiality, parents still worry about the diagnosis of bipolar being a "forever" problem for their child. But your focus should be on what the *disorder* can do to your child, not what the *label* might do. The stigma of mental illness is problematic, but the repercussions of untreated bipolar disorder far exceed whatever difficulties the stigma could bring. This includes the real possibility of suicide.

The greatest problem with the stigma of mental illness is that it makes people avoid treatment. Bipolar disorder must be approached like any chronic medical illness. Although young people have every right to keep their disorder private, I feel encouraged when I hear of cases in which young patients have shared their diagnosis with friends and received their support.

From the beginning of treatment through stabilization, there often is an inverse level of bipolar disorder acceptance between the child and parent. If the parents accept the diagnosis first, the child is less accepting. If the child is fully on board with the diagnosis, the parents are more skeptical. Common scenarios include one parent and the child in a similar level of acceptance compared with the other parent, or one parent fighting an uphill battle to get both the child and the other parent to accept. This can get complicated in divorced and blended families due to the competing opinions and needs among the different households.

There are all kinds of families, containing different personalities and different opinions. Your family may already have challenges that have nothing to do with bipolar disorder. For example, pre-existing problems between parents or teenage oppositional behaviors can further complicate the acceptance of an already difficult mental disorder. As such, the initial focus for parents should be endeavoring to parent effectively and specifically through the bipolar problem. It is helpful for you to remember that bipolar is a genetic disorder that is nobody's fault. You are in no way to blame for your child's condition. Of course, having bipolar isn't your child's fault either, but it's still your child's responsibility to manage this disorder and minimize its problems.

When parents accept the bipolar diagnosis before their child does, the present denial can be regarded as another oppositional act against authority. However, the young patient typically is in denial for the same reasons as adult patients. Kids have lots of fears, too, but adults don't always see those fears openly expressed. Often, young people—especially boys—minimize their internal conflicts. You may have noticed that when you inquire about their problems or feelings, you hear, "I'm fine," or "Yeah, whatever." Many times, the treatment team has to guide them to address their fears while encouraging a sense of emotional safety in doing so. This involves sharing ideas to see how they respond instead of only asking one question after another.

Because bipolar teenagers tend to be more concerned about the reactions of those around them than expressing their own feelings, I frequently tell them, "You probably worry about how your parents react to your moods," and then observe their response. It's not unusual for a kid to perk up and comment, "Yeah, my parents are always freaking out about me." With that, the teen and I have identified a fear to discuss in detail (in this case, the perception of parental overreaction) and an opportunity to gain trust in each other toward acceptance and collaboration.

For you as a parent, it can be difficult to communicate with your child without allowing your own fears to turn into either yelling or just giving up. Sometimes you can use some guidance in helping your child open up through the therapy process. But you can also develop more trust between you and your child with some simple ideas, especially if they're still in denial about bipolar. Using your newfound expertise in bipolar disorder, share some information you've learned about mood swings, and how they can interfere with your child's personal goals. Let children know bipolar is not their fault, but it's important to work together as a family for answers, including how you want to use this opportunity for yourself to be a better parent for them. And through the discussion, listen and acknowledge whatever fears they may be expressing, particularly subtle ones. If you can reflect those fears with the confidence that you're there to help, your chances for success increase together. They can then appreciate how you're there to help them.

But when a teenager accepts bipolar first, the parents can believe their child has too easily latched on to a popular concept. Children are bombarded with influences from many sources, perhaps more than ever in history. Understandably, parents are overwhelmed trying to control these influences. For that reason, those who haven't achieved acceptance can be skeptical to the point of mistrusting professional opinions. They might think bipolar disorder has become a fad or a convenient excuse for impulsivity and failure. They also might be cynical about psychiatry—that is, they believe the profession seeks to medicate kids for an easy profit.

As a parent facing bipolar in your child, you may feel that events around you are moving at a frenetic pace, and you can fear losing control of your child in the process. Instead of being skeptical about bipolar disorder and the people who treat it, try to explore your own fears in the therapy process. Treatment is never about replacing you as the primary authority in your child's life. Along with your child's stabilization through treatment, allow therapy to also meet the goals you strive to achieve on behalf of your son or daughter.

Keeping in mind that bipolar is an explanation, not an excuse, freely discuss your concerns about your child's treatment, and ask how bipolar treatment can address those concerns. Whatever fears you have for your child can likely improve through good bipolar care.

Here are typical fears parents have that bipolar therapy can address:

- Substance use (alcohol and drugs)
- Depression
- Despondency
- Suicidal feelings and actions
- Self-harm/cutting
- Aggression (physical fighting, yelling, profanity, etc.)
- Age-inappropriate sexual activity
- Poor grades
- Poor organization/concentration
- Poor life planning
- Poor social choices
- Disciplinary problems

Treatment might not eliminate all problems at first, but you can expect the immediate symptoms to subside through medication. For example, if your daughter screams and curses at family members with no provocation, with medication for bipolar disorder, she may become less irritable and less easily agitated.

In the stabilization phase of treatment, we look for *less* of things associated with bipolar, namely reducing the bipolar symptoms. Getting both patient and parents through stabilization together takes great effort and patience. Especially with young people, the intensity of the disorder can create numerous problems that require sorting out. Adolescence predictably accelerates everything—emotions, conflicts, growth. Throw bipolar disorder into the mix and life can be chaotic for everyone. It's not unusual for teenage bipolar patients to rapidly cycle through extreme moods—sometimes in a matter of minutes! This volatility requires everyone involved to keep focused squarely on stabilization, giving it as much time and attention as possible. Then in the post-stabilization phase, they can develop coping skills to improve their lives beyond preventing the problems experienced in pre-stabilization.

Treatment also doesn't necessarily turn the parents' lives around right away. During the stabilization phase, lots of resentment among parents and their bipolar children can be evident—and even between the parents themselves. After attempting to raise a child amid fear and unpredictability, it's easy to point fingers. Things are even more complicated in blended families where there are more targets and fingers to point.

It's important for you and the other adults in your child's life to have proper support and education. But remember, it's still your child's responsibility. For young patients who have accepted their disorder, owning bipolar means sharing their thoughts about it with their families and developing a sense of confidence in the journey ahead. Just as they eventually pick a college or start a new job, they're encouraged to take an "adult approach" to their bipolar treatment.

Meanwhile, parents can benefit from couples counseling and, for blended families, family-oriented therapy to improve bonds with each other and work on mutually beneficial goals.

A crucial obstacle for parents during this phase is another layer of denial: *No matter how educated on bipolar they become, all parents want to believe their child can outgrow bipolar disorder.* That's because good parents never want to believe their kids have to suffer something forever.

Bipolar disorder is a chronic illness that requires stabilization and maintenance during the lifelong post-stabilization phase. Parents must know that mood-stabilizing medications can have neuroprotective effects—that is, the medications can actually protect the brain from the damaging effects of untreated mood swings. Although your child can't outgrow bipolar, he or she can manage the disorder effectively throughout his or her lifetime, and meet goals for happiness and success in spite of it.

We also want to start looking for *more* of things in the post-stabilization phase. For kids, therapy focuses on facets of the young person's life that offer gains in relationships, academics, social and recreational choices, and self-esteem. This is when you and your child can go beyond stabilization toward meeting the child's full potential. Unlike patients who first come to bipolar treatment well into their adult years, adolescents who arrive at post-stabilization have a distinct advantage. Because they've had fewer developmental years seeing themselves and the world around them through the distorted lens of mania and depression, forming a healthy and enduring sense of identity is more efficient compared with their adult counterparts. As a parent, you too have an improved chance of establishing better communication with your child, and more opportunities to celebrate life achievements together.

There are some special circumstances with adult children (18 or older). Although technically adults, many remain dependent on their parents to some extent. Their dependence can be material, emotional, or both, and includes those who live on their own or attend college. The challenges for parents in these circumstances center on having less control of their children regarding daily interaction, and less ability to compel them to get treatment.

You might not be sure how involved you should be, and the older the child, the more helpless you can feel. You may be holding on too tightly to your adult child out of fear of the disorder, or you may be distancing yourself out of fear of creating further dependence. In either case, older children can view excessive approaches by their parents as reason to remain in denial and avoid treatment. Finding the right balance of intervention and autonomy can make the greatest difference for a child who has bipolar. A therapist can help negotiate terms between patients and parents while preserving the idea that the patient, no matter what age, needs to take ownership of bipolar more than anyone else.

It's not uncommon for the first identifiable episode of mania or depression to occur during the college years. The pressures of being away from home for the first time—keeping up with schoolwork, meeting new people, lack of sleep, experimentation with recreational drugs, and more—can be catalysts for a serious mood event. College students may need time away from classes and the college milieu to achieve stabilization, especially if the disorder emerges during the school year. I've found that many parents fear that treatment needs will impair their child's ability to complete their studies. If you're the parent of a student who needs treatment now, know that stabilization is the priority, not graduating on time.

Most colleges are increasingly aware of the mental health needs of their students and can provide a medical leave of absence, and help develop disability accommodations when students return to school during post-stabilization. It's also necessary to have a smooth transition to treatment providers who are easily accessible from campus.

Because there's a sense of urgency to return to school as soon as the patient feels better, you can be instrumental in securing every proper resource to help your child reintegrate well into campus life. But don't be afraid to allow time and opportunity to heal, even if it delays graduation. With the right care, your child will have plenty of time to become the success story you've dreamed of.

Caregivers (Adult Children, Adult Siblings, Other Family Members)

Any family member, no matter the relationship, can become fatigued when dealing with a bipolar patient. But the fatigue associated with adult children and other family members who care for a loved one with bipolar is especially high. That's because these caregivers tend to have their own families and multiple other responsibilities in their lives. They also don't usually live full-time with the patient.

As noted earlier, the ideal situation for the involved family member is to be an observer. Caregivers living elsewhere, sometimes miles away, find it difficult to help their bipolar loved ones consistently. For example, a caregiver in one city can work diligently to get an appointment for a psychiatrist set up in another city, only to find out the patient lacked transportation and didn't go. Or perhaps the appointments are successful, but being able to adhere to medication schedules is shaky. Caregivers often feel compelled to call, text, or visit patients all the time just to make sure they're okay, but the constant need for communication always has its limits.

The term "sandwich generation" describes adults who are "sandwiched" between caring for their own children and aging parents. This is even harder for an adult who cares for a bipolar parent, parent figure, or sibling. The spouses and children of the caregiver might show support of these responsibilities at first, but can later feel neglected when the caregiver spends excessive time and energy on the patient's needs. This can create resentments toward caregivers within their own homes and complicate their jobs when using business hours to arrange appointments. The situation is exacerbated when caregivers can't get practical support from other family members, such as their own siblings. A caregiver might complain, "My brother lives closer to Mom, but he refuses to do anything to help."

Also elevating caregiver stress are memories of life growing up with the patient's erratic emotions and behaviors. Memories of manic or depressed parents or siblings may have been repressed for years. In such cases, many people just wanted to leave home, get on with their own lives, and never return to the chaos. Then they suddenly find themselves back in the thick of things.

If you're caring for a bipolar loved one, it's good for you to know that early family conflicts will often resurface. Perhaps you will start reliving deep emotional wounds or have repulsive dreams about fights from years ago. You might argue, curse, or cry when trying to reason with your bipolar loved one. Conflicts with your siblings over how to care for a bipolar parent can regress into petty squabbling. In these situations, caregivers can feel as if they've become the passive "enabler," perhaps like a mother was to a bipolar father. As a result, you also might be harboring huge guilt for wishing you didn't have to be in this position. These and many more thoughts and feelings can erupt along with unconscious resentments and fears you may hold against yourself or project onto your spouse and children.

Caregivers need lots of help. Like other family members, you need to have the emotional turmoil you're experiencing validated and processed. Typically, that requires immediate support in resolving guilt related to the helplessness you feel in the caregiving challenges. Although bipolar disorder is nobody's fault, you may still think you "should be doing more" for your loved one. If this sounds like you, getting education and support from a professional, including individual therapy, can be useful for your emotional relief and a more knowledgeable way forward.

Caregivers who attend educational meetings and therapy sessions often look for specific methods to assist their bipolar loved ones. Ideally, caregiver and patient should attend together and develop a working partnership. However, each situation can require different needs.

In therapy, I invite caregivers to give *their* perspective about their bipolar loved ones and talk about relationships with other family members growing up with bipolar. Those assessments can help determine the caregivers' emotional resources in managing bipolar disorder, especially if it must be done from afar. I believe it's important for you to understand the level of denial or acceptance in your loved one. How much the caregiver's unresolved and unconscious conflicts from early life become reactivated depends initially on the patient's level of denial or acceptance through stabilization. If the denial level is high, that's a much harder hill to climb by yourself.

As a caregiver, find out if you can join your loved one in treatment. This is best done in person, but some therapists now use video teleconferencing to bring everyone together if distance is an issue. Another practical matter to address is identifying one or two other responsible individuals to help out in the caregiving process. This is especially important if your loved one lives alone, but even if they don't, you may find their spouse or roommate to be unreliable. Reach out to other family members or friends and neighbors who understand what living with bipolar is all about, and ask them for help. People identified as potentially helpful may appear reluctant to help—and with good reason. Dealing with bipolar disorder is difficult, and being close by they may have witnessed firsthand the extreme mood swings and the collateral damage. Being empathetic with a reluctant helper is a good idea, but shouldn't stop you from seeking their assistance.

This is particularly necessary with family members who are quite familiar with their loved one with bipolar. Siblings of caregivers can avoid helping for a variety of reasons, some of them sound. If family members genuinely want to help, though, exploring all possibilities of assistance—even modest material support—can go a long way in reducing caregiver stress.

However, if a family member has been living with emotional wounds due to bipolar past or present, then the conversation about assistance takes on a different tone. In cases of estrangement between the patient and a family member, it's important to place his or her reluctance to help in the context of that family member's experience of living with the patient. Try to avoid taking such reluctance personally. And if you take the time to resolve your own early-life conflicts during therapy, you'll be in a good position to have more productive conversations with your siblings and other family members.

A family member might avoid helping the person with bipolar directly but be amenable to assisting the caregiver. This possibility gets overlooked when old wounds, intense frustrations, and reduced trust get in the way. For example, an exasperated caregiver could tell a sibling, "I'm so stressed out, and you haven't done anything for Mom." Certainly, that sibling should hear the cry for help as serious, but this kind of statement brings out anger and guilt from the past. Knowing the sibling's anxiety about getting involved with the bipolar parent, the caregiver might say, "I know how hard it is to deal with Mom. So instead of helping her, I'd appreciate it if you could help *me*. I have the number for the local Dial-a-Ride to get her to her doctor's appointments. Could you call and find out the schedules for me?"

If you as a caregiver can break down your needs into small, attainable parts, you can begin a simple program to solicit help from others. You'll soon discover this approach can be less threatening than making demands, and although it takes time, you'll feel less burdened by every weighty detail.

Caregivers by nature do not ask for help freely—at least not initially—and that may be the case with you. It may seem easier to do everything yourself rather than feel guilty about burdening others. This behavior might be a holdover from childhood. Maybe you were the responsible older sibling, and now family members silently expect you to repeat the pattern through adulthood. But you're not that child anymore and you need to ask for help. Not doing so can lead to resentment, anger, and burnout. Providing specific requests for assistance can reverse any pattern of non-involvement in a family.

If you are taking care of a bipolar loved one, one important factor to consider is power of attorney and conservatorship or guardianship. We expect bipolar patients from youth to old age to take ownership of their illness. As the years go on, though, they can become increasingly dependent due to aging and the disease progressing. As this reality presents itself, the caregiver benefits from understanding local laws governing power of attorney and conservatorship or guardianship (which means essentially the same thing in different states).

In general, having a power of attorney permits the patient to designate the caregiver as the legal medical decision maker on his or her behalf. The court grants conservatorship or guardianship when patients are incapable of making decisions on their own. This grants the caregiver full authority over the patient's daily life. This may seem like an extreme measure, but when

patients are severely and permanently disabled by bipolar disorder, going to court to assume full rights over that person's life may
be the last option available.

It's important for you to understand your loved one's legal,
medical, and financial aspects. Consulting with an attorney who
specializes in this area is a good place to start.

For All Family Members

Getting family involved in all three phases of treatment is critical.
In pre-stabilization, an initial intervention—especially with two
or three family members on hand—can help patients understand
how bipolar disorder affects them and the people around them.
Each family member can contribute a different dimension to
these effects and offer support in unique ways. During stabilization, family helps by remaining positive and encouraging through
medication trials and the anxiety of what changes follow.

But involvement can be most critical in the post-stabilization
phase. Prescribing the right medications and preparing an overall
treatment plan for long-term management doesn't mean the task
is finished. Post-stabilization is when deep therapy work on life
and relationships begins. Because patients require time and opportunity during post-stabilization to develop a complete sense
of who they are separate from their bipolar disorder, family members need to discover what the true character of the bipolar
patient is really all about. As a family member of a bipolar patient,
it will be challenging for you to know if the emotions and behaviors you're witnessing are from bipolar disorder or reflect the real
person inside.

If the person with bipolar is upset, having a bad day, or genuinely excited about something, you might wonder if the bipolar
symptoms have returned. It's common to think, "Is she off her
meds?" or "He seems way too happy about this." Maybe in the
middle of an argument, you might actually say, "Have you told

your doctor about your anger?" These and similar concerns can be reasonable, but having an overarching principle to guide conversations through the uncertainties of post-stabilization is necessary.

During the post-stabilization phase of bipolar therapy, I help family members and patients learn and practice what I call the Grand Bargain. Each participant holds up one end of the bargain: For the family member, it is *I won't think everything about you is bipolar disorder if I know you're keeping your disease under control.* For the patient, it is *I will always keep you updated about my disease as long as you don't think everything about me is bipolar disorder.*

Patients and family members don't always see eye to eye on how each keeps up with the bargain; what's important is they're free to remind each other of the bargain's constancy in their lives. Occasional conversations about bipolar management and discoveries of who the patient "really is" can be enough to keep the Grand Bargain in force. Likewise, you should feel at liberty to reinforce progress in your bipolar loved one and point out your concerns.

It should be permissible for you to say something such as, "You've been doing great with managing your bipolar, but you've been getting more irritable lately. What's going on?" This statement doesn't try to curtail the possible influence of bipolar, but it does open up the conversation about what could be causing the symptoms (irritability in this example).

If the response is something like, "Yeah, work has been getting pretty stressful and I don't know how I'm going to meet my deadlines," then there's a real-life circumstance to discuss. Perhaps it's an opportunity to find out more about that "real person" apart from bipolar as well as how best the situation can be handled while remaining in a baseline mood zone.

If the response lacks immediate information or the patient seems surprised by this feedback, you might follow up with, "Even though you've been doing well, maybe changes are going on inside that we need to talk about." This can be an emotionally safe and productive exchange if the Grand Bargain has been in effect and well-practiced.

The Grand Bargain remains through the long phase of disease management while giving everyone involved the confidence to address reasonable concerns head-on. It also can give patients a sense of freedom to explore who they're meant to be. Post-stabilization means patients will have periods of joy and sorrow along with frustration and triumph. It doesn't eliminate the likelihood of occasional periods of hypomania or dysthymia. As long as they don't cycle repeatedly in and out of the mood zones adjoining the baseline, this can be considered the "new normal" for any person with bipolar disorder. Perhaps that person can say to the loved one, "I do feel I'm moving in those zones at times, but I'm taking my medications, discussing it with my therapist, and owning it for the long haul. I don't think it's a problem, but let me know if you feel it's getting out of hand."

Both patient and family need to exercise patience as they distinguish the "you" or "me" from the bipolar. It can take months or years to fully understand.

Family members ultimately are challenged to accept all changes that come with treatment and some changes that may never happen. Treatment affords good opportunities but won't make a person with bipolar "perfect."

This sounds obvious, but it might surprise you how vigorously expectations can be assigned, especially when things at one time were terrible. It's easy to neglect gratitude and focus instead on things that didn't change to your liking. If bipolar is well managed, then the person with bipolar has the opportunity to be that wonderfully flawed individual people learn to love all over again.

Social and Community Supports

Beyond the personal involvement of family, people with bipolar disorder also need a sense of belonging from the community.

This may come from schools, churches, places of work, mental health groups, twelve-step groups (if addiction is an issue), volunteer organizations, or recreational or social clubs. Even if no one else in these groups knows about the person's bipolar disorder, any place where that person feels a welcome presence can promote a healthy sense of accountability to the world. When people with bipolar extend their presence to others, they learn they possess unique and honest gifts to contribute to causes greater than themselves.

In this realm, they understand at a deep level that the grandiosity of mania did nothing to change the world and neither did their avoidance of others during depression. Instead, they offer their talents and warmth to others in exchange for validation of their beautiful individuality. This social and spiritual connectivity is essential in believing that owning bipolar is not only a commitment to self and family, it's also a commitment to the larger world in which they belong.

Working with Families and Knowing When to Let Go

Despite our best efforts to encourage, support, cajole, or threaten people with bipolar into treatment, it is their singular responsibility to *own* bipolar disorder. When they're confused or disoriented from the severe effects of the condition, we can't expect them to take immediate responsibility. However, at reasonable points, it is *their* disease to own, no matter the age or severity. As mentioned earlier, the family should not work harder to own bipolar than the patient does. The patient has to become the captain of the ship because ultimately no one can force treatment on her or him. This is true for adolescents, adult children, elderly people, and patients who have been hospitalized. Being forcefully compelled to start treatment has its limits; bipolar ownership is mandatory.

What if the patient refuses to own bipolar? How long do you have to wait? Where do you draw the line and say, "Enough is enough"?

These may be the most difficult questions to ponder. The answers depend on the unique circumstances in each relationship. Spouses who have struggled through the effects of mania and depression, then battled to get their bipolar loved ones to treatment, may explore separation or divorce. Parents may feel all their challenges with their bipolar children have come down to allowing them to sink or swim on their own. Caregivers might conclude they no longer can jeopardize their marriages or relationships with other loved ones to care for a recalcitrant bipolar parent or sibling. These are painful, agonizing decisions, but at times, such decisions must be made.

In our journey to own bipolar, we will do the very best together in seeking ways to help the bipolar patient break through denial, and find a pathway to reach the "real person" inside. But, we are also just as invested in the whole family's mental health. No family member has an infinite capacity for the psychological effects of their loved one's mood swings, and they can't be expected to accept an entire life of misery and fear. When all options are exhausted and one's conscience is clear, it's reasonable—perhaps imperative—to let go of that person with bipolar disorder.

If you are weighing this most difficult decision, it's common to either fear your bipolar loved one will get *worse* without you or get *better* without you. The former outcome could mean that loved one might free-fall into despair without your support. The latter could mean all the work to separate permanently would be regretted if he or she gets bipolar treatment later in life.

Some people only get better after they've undergone consequences, such as a divorce. What both scenarios suggest is that the patient was overly dependent on you, and could not or would not own bipolar while being so dependent. Sometimes in life we just have to learn things the hard way.

As a therapist, I don't recommend a patient "hit bottom" just because nothing else seems to work; that's a dangerous approach.

But I'd be remiss in not recognizing that a penchant for denial is embedded in our humanity. Helping family members cope with this reality is at times the only viable approach for them to achieve peace in their lives. And it might be true that letting go would be the only way for the person with bipolar to ultimately own the disease.

At times, the need to let go must come *from* the bipolar patient *to* the family member. Sometimes people with bipolar disorder already have alienated their spouses, parents, or entire families due to their untreated illness. Or their families refuse to become a part of treatment, thereby creating a sense of abandonment. Either way, if you're that person with bipolar, you may feel that you've lost a big reason to pursue or maintain treatment. Supposedly, the most dangerous person is the one who has nothing left to lose.

But the alternative is that with nothing left to lose, you have so much more to gain. I have known people with bipolar who courageously pursue treatment, even with no family around them, and eventually discover a new life—with new people they can love and who can love them in return.

If you have let go of a bipolar loved one, or you're struggling with bipolar by yourself, treatment and support remain within reach. If you can follow a treatment path while grieving aspects of your former life, then fully owning bipolar can create an exciting new way for you to live—free from the fears that have bound you to the past. As the great psychoanalyst Sigmund Freud said, "One day, in retrospect, the years of struggle will strike you as the most beautiful."[5]

Notes

1. Miklowitz, D. J. (2006). A review of evidence-based psychosocial interventions for bipolar disorder. *Journal of Clinical Psychiatry, 67*(Suppl 11), 28–33.

2. Pernice-Duca, F. (2010). Family network support and mental health recovery. *Journal of Marital & Family Therapy, 36*(1), 13–27.
3. Pipich, M. (Ed.) (2013). The bipolar network's shared stories. Retrieved December 1, 2013, from http://bipolarnetwork.com/shared-stories.html
4. Ibid.
5. Freud, Sigmund (1907). Letter to C. G. Jung.

CONCLUSION

· · · · · · ·

Going to the Next Level

THE PRECEDING CHAPTERS BROKE DOWN bipolar disorder into its many parts—from its historical, genetic, and neurological foundations to how it manifests itself in manic and depressive symptoms, and then finally to how individual and family treatments progress through the three phases of bipolar therapy. Examining these components not only serves our knowledge on the subject, it replaces fears of misunderstanding and ignorance with a newfound confidence based in the pursuit of truth.

Congratulations! You have learned much and have become a true expert in owning bipolar. Now it's time to graduate to the next level. The Greek philosopher Aristotle is credited with saying, "The whole is more than the sum of its parts."[1] That means we piece together all the parts of what we've learned to produce something bigger and better for all. For our purposes, two components of success reside in the greater whole of owning bipolar—that is, personal action and helping others.

Personal Action

Our elevated awareness and knowledge require that we take action. Ideas are lifeless without our passionate pursuit for change. Owning bipolar isn't simply an internal activity of acceptance. It's meant to reach forward to do what we need to accomplish outside ourselves. It isn't only accepting the truth about bipolar, it's about assertively living that truth for ourselves *and* for those around us.

And what is always said about the truth?

- It hurts.
- It will set you free.

Reading this book, you may have thought about an important truth you painfully struggle to face—some avoided truth that has kept you chained in fear. It could be a truth about yourself, about someone you know, or both. You might have felt inadequate because of the initial lack of knowledge.

Ignorance no longer rules you. Maybe you've feared your loved one's denial. But now you can tackle the uncertainties that belie it. Perhaps you've delayed confronting bipolar because you've worried about alienation or condemnation. But you don't care about those things anymore because you're emboldened to save someone's life. And the life you save could be your own.

Helping Others

That leads to the second component—helping others. With your knowledge, empowerment to change, and full bipolar ownership, you can help someone in the future who's struggling with mental illness. Trust me, it will happen. It won't matter how open or private you are with your own story. Too many people in the world are suffering silently, aimlessly, and in isolation, just as you have.

Owning bipolar changes you into a more empathetic person of action. While you're fully accountable to your own mental illness, no longer can you ignore suffering around you, especially when it's presented in subtle ways. The highest level of bipolar ownership is carrying forward your wisdom to those who need it. Be assured they will tell you—one way or another—how desperately they need your guidance.

Society values individual freedom and an individual's right to privacy. That's good, of course. But there are times when you'll witness a type of communication from another person—direct or indirect—and recognize it all too well. It's a reaching out from someone who may indeed sense your ability to manage truth surrounded by fear. Perhaps a neighbor gently complains about living with an emotionally troubled adolescent. Or perhaps a coworker is displaying uncharacteristic behavioral changes in your presence. Or out of the blue, a complete stranger needs a sympathetic ear and seeks your confidence to reassess his or her direction. Embrace these sudden, often fleeting chances to listen, share, and guide. Maybe you can provide understanding, comfort, or even a professional referral. But no matter the circumstances, you will be prepared for the moment.

As you cross paths with people who can benefit from your understanding and inner strength, you will experience the greater whole with each person you touch. And in each precious moment, you will renew your commitment to owning bipolar in your life. As they reach out to you, you'll discover that embedded in every cry for help is the opportunity to share a single truth that has set you free.

"Don't be afraid," you will say. "You are not alone."

Notes

1. Aristotle. (1896). *Metaphysics.* (John H. M'Mahon, Trans). London: George Bell and Sons. (Original work published in 350 BCE).

Reference Guide
to Bipolar Medications
• • • • • • • • • • • • • • • • •

How to Use This Guide

This is a basic reference guide to the bipolar disorder medications discussed in this book. The information here gives you a basic understanding of those medications and what you can expect from them. It is *not* intended to be a complete psychiatric guide, nor should it replace information or recommendations from a prescribing physician. The intention is to present fundamental information in a simple format so bipolar patients and families can better discuss medications with the appropriate medical specialists toward successfully owning bipolar.

The information presented is pertinent mostly to adult patients. Young children and geriatric patients may require different approaches in specific medication choices, dosages, and overall management. Also, some of these medications may be available in extended or controlled-release formulas, which may make them more tolerable. Consult your doctor for all potential differences.

You are encouraged to use this guide to form questions for your medical team. If you notice any problems before or after you or your loved one begins bipolar medications, direct your questions, concerns, or ideas to those specialists. Be sure to mention all the medications you're taking now, along with any psychiatric medications you may have taken previously. It's also wise to include a history of any medication sensitivities, substance abuse issues, brain injury, or metabolic problems such as hypothyroidism or diabetes. You may also want to inform them of any known liver, kidney, or pancreas problems, and convey how you feel about getting blood serum tests. If you are a female patient, let them know if you might be pregnant or plan on becoming pregnant in the near future.

Also know that side effects presented in this book are divided into "Common" and "Uncommon" for ease of understanding and expectation. It's important to discuss side effects of all types with your medical team, especially when starting a medication or increasing its dosage. Note that not all side effects or warnings/precautions are listed on the pages that follow.

Note: All brand names listed are registered trademarks.

Mood Stabilizers—Lithium

GENERIC NAMES: Lithium, lithium carbonate

BRAND NAMES: Eskalith, Lithonate, Lithobid, Lithane, Lithotabs

BIPOLAR USAGE: First-line for acute mania/hypomania (during or
following a recent manic/hypomanic episode) and long-
term maintenance

MAIN EFFECTS: Reduction in manic/hypomanic symptoms and prevention of bipolar depressive symptoms

SIDE EFFECTS, COMMON: Mild thirst, fine hand tremor, excessive urination, mild nausea, mild headache

SIDE EFFECTS, UNCOMMON: More severe or persistent of the above,
gastrointestinal problems (diarrhea, vomiting, gastritis,
etc.), blurred vision, dizziness, sexual dysfunction, weight
gain or loss, neuromuscular problems (slurred speech,
poor muscle control, twitching, etc.), skin problems (acne-
like lesions, rash, etc.), hair loss, seizures, kidney failure,
and others

WARNINGS/PRECAUTIONS: Pregnancy, breastfeeding, history of kidney or heart disease, history of brain damage, severe dehydration

TYPICAL DOSAGE, RANGES: Acute mania/hypomania: 1200–2400 mg per day

MAINTENANCE: 600–800 mg per day

BLOOD SERUM LEVEL: 0.6–1.50 mEq/L

Mood Stabilizers—Anticonvulsant/Antiseizure

GENERIC NAMES: Divalproex, divalproex sodium, valproate, vaproic acid, sodium valproate

BRAND NAMES: Depakote, Depakene

BIPOLAR USAGE: First-line for acute mania/hypomania, rapid cycling, and mixed episodes

MAIN EFFECTS: Reduction in manic/hypomanic symptoms, especially with dysphoric irritability

SIDE EFFECTS, COMMON: Mild thirst, fine hand tremor, mild diarrhea, constipation, mild nausea, mild headache, drowsiness

SIDE EFFECTS, UNCOMMON: More severe or persistent effects stated above, gastrointestinal problems (diarrhea, vomiting, gastritis, etc.), dizziness, bleeding or bruising, weight gain or loss, muscle weakness, yellowing of eyes or skin, hair loss, confusion

WARNINGS/PRECAUTIONS: Pregnancy, breastfeeding, history of liver or pancreatic disease, risk of polycystic ovary syndrome (PCOS)

TYPICAL DOSAGE, RANGE: 750–1500 mg per day

BLOOD SERUM LEVEL: 50–100 mcg/ml

GENERIC NAME: Carbamazepine

BRAND NAMES: Tegretol, Equatro

BIPOLAR USAGE: First-line for mixed episodes, second-line for acute mania/hypomania

MAIN EFFECTS: Reduction in manic/hypomanic symptoms, especially with dysphoric irritability

SIDE EFFECTS, COMMON: Mild thirst, fine hand tremor, mild diarrhea, mild nausea, mild headache, drowsiness

SIDE EFFECTS, UNCOMMON: More severe or persistent effects stated above, gastrointestinal problems (diarrhea, vomiting, gastritis, etc.), dizziness, weight gain or loss, muscle weakness, yellowing of eyes or skin, hair loss, confusion, increased psychosis (especially in younger patients), skin problems (rash, hives, etc.), bleeding or bruising, blurred vision, irregular heartbeat, confusion

WARNINGS/PRECAUTIONS: Pregnancy, breastfeeding, history of significant liver or pancreatic disease, or diabetes

TYPICAL DOSAGE, RANGE: 600–1600 mg per day

BLOOD SERUM LEVEL: 4–12 mcg/ml

GENERIC NAME: Lamotrigine

BRAND NAME: Lamictal

BIPOLAR USAGE: First-line for bipolar depression (without recent mania/hypomania) and long-term maintenance; can be added to an existing antimanic medication

MAIN EFFECTS: Reduction in acute depressive bipolar symptoms, prevention of bipolar depressive symptoms

SIDE EFFECTS, COMMON: Mild thirst, fine hand tremor, mild diarrhea, constipation, mild nausea, mild headache, insomnia

SIDE EFFECTS, UNCOMMON: More severe or persistent effects stated above, vomiting, bleeding or bruising, skin problems (especially rash or hives, such as Stevens-Johnson syndrome), fever, shortness of breath

WARNINGS/PRECAUTIONS: Pregnancy, breastfeeding, history of significant liver or kidney disease, Stevens-Johnson syndrome (a potentially lethal skin disease, marked by flu-like symptoms and a red to purplish rash)

DOSAGE RANGE: 50–500 mg

BLOOD SERUM LEVEL: Generally, a blood test is not needed.

Other Common Mood Stabilizers

GENERIC NAME: Topiramate

BRAND NAME: Topamax

BIPOLAR USAGE: First-line for acute mania/hypomania, rapid cycling and mixed episodes

MAIN EFFECTS: Reduction in manic/hypomanic symptoms, especially with dysphoric irritability, migraine headache prevention; may be better for weight control compared to other medications

SIDE EFFECTS, COMMON: Mild thirst, fine hand tremor, mild diarrhea, constipation, mild nausea, drowsiness

SIDE EFFECTS, UNCOMMON: More severe or persistent effects stated above, gastrointestinal problems (diarrhea, vomiting, gastritis, etc.), dizziness, bleeding or bruising, weight gain or loss, muscle weakness, yellowing of eyes or skin, hair loss, confusion

WARNINGS/PRECAUTIONS: Pregnancy, breastfeeding, history of liver or pancreatic disease

DOSAGE RANGE: 750–1500 mg per day

BLOOD SERUM LEVEL: 50–100 mcg/ml

GENERIC NAME: Oxcarbazepine

BRAND NAME: Trileptal

BIPOLAR USAGE: Acute mania/hypomania, rapid cycling and mixed episodes

MAIN EFFECTS: Reduction in manic/hypomanic symptoms, chemically similar to carbamazepine, but known to be often better tolerated with fewer side effects in most patients

SIDE EFFECTS, COMMON: Mild thirst, fine hand tremor, mild diarrhea, mild nausea, mild headache, drowsiness

SIDE EFFECTS, UNCOMMON: More severe or persistent effects stated above, gastrointestinal problems (diarrhea, vomiting, gastritis, etc.), dizziness, weight gain or loss, muscle weakness, yellowing of eyes or skin, hair loss, confusion, increased psychosis (especially in younger patients), skin problems (rash, hives, etc.), bleeding or bruising, blurred vision, irregular heartbeat, confusion

WARNINGS/PRECAUTIONS: Pregnancy, breastfeeding, history of liver or pancreatic disease

DOSAGE RANGE: 300–2400 mg per day

BLOOD SERUM LEVEL: 3–35 mcg/ml

GENERIC NAME: Gabapentin

BRAND NAME: Neurontin

BIPOLAR USAGE: Acute mania/hypomania, bipolar depression, and maintenance (overall use for bipolar is controversial due to a lack of scientific evidence)

MAIN EFFECTS: Reduction in manic/hypomanic and bipolar depressive symptoms; also may improve neuropathy (nerve pain)

SIDE EFFECTS, COMMON: Mild thirst, fine hand tremor, mild diarrhea, mild nausea, mild headache, drowsiness

SIDE EFFECTS, UNCOMMON: More severe or persistent effects stated above, gastrointestinal problems (diarrhea, vomiting, gastritis, etc.), dizziness, weight gain or loss, muscle weakness, yellowing of eyes or skin, hair loss, confusion, increased psychosis (especially in younger patients), skin problems (rash, hives, etc.), bleeding or bruising, blurred vision, irregular heartbeat, confusion, rapid eye movements

WARNINGS/PRECAUTIONS: Pregnancy, breastfeeding, history of liver or pancreatic disease

DOSAGE RANGE: 300–4800 mg per day
BLOOD SERUM TEST: 2.0–20.0 mcg/ml

Atypical (Second-Generation) Antipsychotics—
Antimanic, Antidepressive, Maintenance

Antimanic

GENERIC NAME	BRAND NAMES	TYPICAL DOSAGE RANGE (PER DAY)
Aripiprazole	Abilify	15–30 mg
Asenapine	Saphris	10–20 mg
Cariprazine	Vraylar	3–6 mg
Clozapine	Clozaril	300–900 mg
Olanzapine	Zyprexa	5–20 mg
Paliperidone	Invega	3–12 mg
Risperidone	Risperdal	4–16 mg
Quetiapine	Seroquel	300–750 mg
Ziprasodone	Geodon	60–160 mg

BIPOLAR USAGE: First- or second-line for acute mania/hypomania and/or mixed episodes, especially when severe and/or accompanied by psychotic symptoms (e.g., hallucinations, delusional thinking); can be added to certain other bipolar medications

MAIN EFFECTS: Reduction in manic/hypomanic and psychotic symptoms

Antidepressive

GENERIC NAME	BRAND NAMES	TYPICAL DOSAGE RANGE (PER DAY)
Lurasidone	Latuda	40–80 mg
Quetiapine	Seroquel	300–750 mg

BIPOLAR USAGE: First- or second-line for bipolar depressive symptoms and mixed episodes, especially when severe and/or accompanied by psychotic symptoms (e.g., hallucinations, delusional thinking); can be added to certain other bipolar medications

MAIN EFFECTS: Reduction in bipolar depressive symptoms and psychotic symptoms

Maintenance

GENERIC NAME	BRAND NAMES	TYPICAL DOSAGE RANGE (PER DAY)
Aripiprazole	Abilify	15–30 mg
Olanzapine	Zyprexa	5–20 mg
Quetiapine	Seroquel	300–750 mg
Ziprasodone	Geodon	60–160 mg

BIPOLAR USAGE: Long-term maintenance for the prevention of symptom relapse, often paired with certain other bipolar medications

MAIN EFFECTS: Prevention of manic/hypomanic, bipolar depressive, and psychotic symptoms

Typical (First-Generation) Antipsychotics—Low Potency, High Potency

Low Potency

GENERIC NAME	BRAND NAMES	TYPICAL DOSAGE RANGE (PER DAY)
Chlorpromazine	Thorazine	50–1500 mg
Thioridazine	Mellaril	150–800 mg

High Potency

GENERIC NAME	BRAND NAMES	TYPICAL DOSAGE RANGE (PER DAY)
Fluphenazine	Prolixin	3–45 mg
Haloperidol	Haldol	2–40 mg
Loxapine	Loxitane	50–250 mg
Thiothiazine	Navane	10–60 mg
Perphenazine	Trilafon	8–60 mg
Pimozide	Orap	1–10 mg
Trifluoperazine	Stelazine	10–40 mg

BIPOLAR USAGE: Primarily for acute mania/hypomania and/or mixed episodes, especially when severe and/or accompanied by psychotic symptoms (e.g., hallucinations, delusional thinking); can be added to certain other bipolar medications. Can also be used for bipolar depression. Commonly used third-line or below due to higher side-effect profile compared to second-generation antipsychotics.

MAIN EFFECTS: Reduction in manic/hypomanic and psychotic symptoms

Antipsychotics—Side Effects

SIDE EFFECTS, COMMON: Mild thirst, fine hand tremor, constipation, mild dizziness, breast enlargement or discharge, sexual dysfunction, weight gain

SIDE EFFECTS, UNCOMMON: More severe or persistent effects stated above, gastrointestinal problems, stupor, neuromuscular problems (slurred speech, poor muscle control, twitching, etc.), skin problems (discoloration), light sensitivity, urination problems, fever, changes in blood pressure, seizures, shortness of breath

WARNINGS/PRECAUTIONS: Pregnancy, breastfeeding, history of kidney or liver disease, or metabolic disease such as diabetes

Antidepressants—SSRI and SNRI

Selective Serotonin Reuptake Inhibitors (SSRI)

GENERIC NAME	BRAND NAMES	TYPICAL DOSAGE RANGE (PER DAY)
Citalopram	Celexa	10–40 mg
Escitalopram	Lexapro	5–20 mg
Fluoxetine	Prozac	20–80 mg
Fluvoxamine	Luvox	50–300 mg
Paroxetine	Paxil	20–60 mg
Sertraline	Zoloft	50–200 mg
Vilazodone	Viibryd	10–40 mg

Serotonin and Norepinephrine Reuptake Inhibitors (SNRI)

GENERIC NAME	BRAND NAMES	TYPICAL DOSAGE RANGE (PER DAY)
Desvenlafaxine	Pristiq	50–400 mg
Duloxetine	Cymbalta	40–60 mg
Levomilnacipran	Fetzima	20–120 mg
Venlafaxine	Effexor	75–350 mg

BIPOLAR USAGE: Second-line or below for bipolar depressive symptoms, typically paired with an antimanic medication to avoid becoming catalytic for mania/hypomania

MAIN EFFECTS: Reduction and prevention of bipolar depressive symptoms

Antidepressants—Atypical

GENERIC NAME	BRAND NAMES	TYPICAL DOSAGE RANGE (PER DAY)
Bupropion	Wellbutrin	150–300 mg
Mirtazapine	Remeron	15–45 mg
Vortioxetine	Trintellix, Brintellix	5–20 mg

BIPOLAR USAGE: Bipolar depressive symptoms typically paired with an antimanic medication to avoid becoming catalytic for mania/hypomania; caution should be used when a history of psychotic symptoms is evident

MAIN EFFECTS: Reduction and prevention of bipolar depressive symptoms

Antidepressants—TCA and MAOI

TCA (Tricyclics)

GENERIC NAME	BRAND NAMES	TYPICAL DOSAGE RANGE (PER DAY)
Amitriptyline	Elavil	75–300 mg
Amoxepine	Asendin	150–400 mg
Clomipramine	Anafranil	75–200 mg
Desipramine	Norpramine	75–300 mg
Doxepin	Sinequan	75–300 mg
Imipramine	Tofranil	75–300 mg
Maprotiline	Ludiomil	75–225 mg
Nefazodone	Serzone	100–600 mg
Nortriptyline	Pamelor	50–150 mg
Protriptyline	Vivactil	15–60 mg
Trazodone	Desyrel	150–400 mg
Trimipramine	Surmontil	75–300 mg

Monoamine Oxidase Inhibitors (MAOI)

GENERIC NAME	BRAND NAMES	TYPICAL DOSAGE RANGE (PER DAY)
Isocarboxazid	Marplan	10–40 mg
Phenelzine	Nardil	30–90 mg
Selegiline	Emsam	6–12 mg (transdermal)
Traylcypromine	Parnate	20–60 mg

BIPOLAR USAGE: Third-line or below for bipolar depressive symptoms typically paired with an antimanic medication. However, these medications are usually more catalytic for mania/hypomania and have poorer drug interactions than other antidepressants, especially with MAOI.

MAIN EFFECTS: Reduction and prevention of bipolar depressive symptoms

Antidepressants—Side Effects

Note: There are many side effect differences among the antidepressant classes. What is listed here represents those in the most commonly prescribed antidepressants for bipolar disorder. Remember that some side effects are more present or pronounced in certain medications than other choices. Your doctor can explain these specific differences for you.

SIDE EFFECTS, COMMON: Mild thirst, mild nausea, mild dizziness, mild headache, diarrhea, constipation, agitation, drowsiness, insomnia, sexual dysfunction

SIDE EFFECTS, UNCOMMON: More severe or persistent effects stated above, weight gain or loss, changes in appetite, blurred vision, hand tremor, chills or fever, light sensitivity, skin problems (rash, hives, or discoloration), shortness of breath, sedation, bleeding or bruising, blood pressure changes, increased suicidal thoughts, seizures

WARNINGS/PRECAUTIONS: History or evidence of mania/hypomania, increased suicidal thoughts (especially in younger patients), increased psychotic symptoms, pregnancy, breastfeeding, history of kidney or liver disease, history of seizures

Antianxiety/Anxiolytics—
Benzodiazepines and Hypnotics

Benzodiazepines

GENERIC NAME	BRAND NAMES	TYPICAL DOSAGE RANGE (PER DAY)
Alprazolem	Xanax	0.5–6 mg
Chlordiazepoxide	Librium	15–100 mg
Clonazepam	Klonopin	1–8 mg
Clorazepate	Tranxene	7.5–60 mg
Diazepam	Valium	4–40 mg
Flurazepam	Dalmane	15–60 mg
Lorazepam	Ativan	1.5–6 mg
Oxazepam	Serax	30–90 mg
Prazepam	Centrax	20–40 mg
Temazepam	Restoril	15–60 mg
Triazolam	Halcion	0.125–0.5 mg

Hypnotics

GENERIC NAME	BRAND NAMES	TYPICAL DOSAGE RANGE (PER DAY)
Estazolam	ProSom	1–2 mg
Eszopidone	Lunesta	1–3 mg
Zaleplon	Sonata	5–10 mg
Zolpidem	Ambien	5–10 mg

BIPOLAR USAGE: Anxiety, irritability, sleep disturbances, excitement in mania/hypomania, especially dysphoric mania/hypomania, and in bipolar depression

MAIN EFFECTS: Reduction and prevention of anxiety, irritability, and sleep disturbances

SIDE EFFECTS, COMMON: Mild nausea, mild dizziness, drowsiness

SIDE EFFECTS, UNCOMMON: More severe or persistent effects stated above, confusion, forgetfulness, slurred speech, skin problems (rash or hives), swelling of hands or feet

WARNINGS/PRECAUTIONS: Pregnancy, breastfeeding, history of liver or kidney disease, risk of tolerance and dependence (addiction). Discontinuation should be managed by a physician due to possible withdrawal syndrome or seizures.

Antianxiety/Anxiolytics—Buspirone, Antihistamines, and Beta-Blockers

Buspirone

GENERIC NAME	BRAND NAMES	TYPICAL DOSAGE RANGE (PER DAY)
Buspirone	BuSpar	10–40 mg

Antihistamines

GENERIC NAME	BRAND NAMES	TYPICAL DOSAGE RANGE (PER DAY)
Diphenhydramine	Benadryl	75–200 mg
Hydroxyzine	Atarax, Vistaril	30–200 mg

Beta-Blockers

GENERIC NAME	BRAND NAMES	TYPICAL DOSAGE RANGE (PER DAY)
Atenolol	Tenormin	25–100 mg
Propranolol	Inderal	20–160 mg

BIPOLAR USAGE: Anxiety, irritability, sleep disturbances, excitement in mania/hypomania, especially dysphoric mania/hypomania, and in bipolar depression

MAIN EFFECTS: Reduction and prevention of anxiety, irritability and sleep disturbances

SIDE EFFECTS, COMMON: Mild nausea, mild dizziness, drowsiness

SIDE EFFECTS, UNCOMMON: More severe or persistent effects stated above, confusion, forgetfulness, and others depending on the specific medication and its use

WARNINGS/PRECAUTIONS: Pregnancy, breastfeeding, history of liver or kidney disease

Medication Guide References

Bilo, L., & Meo, R. (2008) Polycystic ovary syndrome in women using valproate: A review. *Gynecol Endrocrinol, 24*(10), 562–570.

British Psychological Society (2006). *Bipolar disorder: The management of bipolar disorder in adults, children and adolescents, in primary and secondary care.* Leicester, UK: Author.

Calabrese, J. R., Keck, P. E., Starace, A., Lu, K., Ruth, A., Laszlovszky I., et al. (2015). Efficacy and safety of low- and high-dose cariprazine in acute and mixed mania associated with Bipolar I Disorder: A double-blind, placebo-controlled study. *Journal of Clinical Psychiatry, 76*(3), 284–292.

Crismon, M. L., Argo, T. R., Bendele, S. D., & Suppes, T. (2007). *Texas medication algorithm project procedural manual: Bipolar disorder algorithms.* Austin, TX: Texas Department of State Health Services.

Hirschfeld, R. M., Bowden, C. L., Gitlin, M. J., Keck, P. E., Suppes, T., Thase, M. E., et al. (2010). *Practice guideline for the treatment of patients with bipolar disorder* (2nd ed.). Arlington, VA: American Psychiatric Association.

Konstantinos, F. N., Kontis, D., Gonda, X., Siamouli, M., & Yatham, L. N. (2012). Treatment of mixed bipolar states. *International Journal of Neuropsychopharmacology, 15*(7), 1015–1026.

Liu, M. T., Maroney, M. E., & Hermes-DeSantis, E. R. (2015). Levomilnacipran and vortioxetine: Review of new phamacotherapies for major depressive disorder. *World Journal of Pharmacology, 4*(1), 17–30.

Loebel, A., Cucchiaro, J., Silva, R., Kroger, H., Hsu, J., Sarma, K., & Sachs, G. (2014). Lurasidone monotherapy in the treatment of bipolar I depression: A randomized, double-blind, placebo controlled study. *American Journal of Psychiatry, 171*(2), 160–168.

McElroy, S. L., Keck, P. E., & Post, R. M. (Ed.) (2008). *Antiepileptic drugs to treat psychiatric disorders.* New York: Informa Healthcare USA.

Northamptonshire Healthcare (2007). Guidelines for the monitoring of antimanic and prophylactic medication in bipolar disorder. NHT Policy Number MM-G-023. Retrieved September 30, 2016, from http://neneccg.nhs.uk/resources

Pacchiarotti, I., Bond, D. J., Baldessarini, R. J., Nolen, W. A., Grunze, H., Licht, R. W., et al. (2013). The international society for bipolar disorders (ISBD) task force report on antidepressant use in bipolar disorders. *American Journal of Psychiatry, 170*(11), 1249–1262.

Preston, J. D., O'Neal, J. H., & Talaga, M. C. (2013). *Handbook of clinical psychopharmacology for therapists* (7th ed.). Oakland, CA: New Harbinger Publications.

Renk, K., White, R., Lauer, B-A, McSwiggan, M., Puff, J., & Lowell, A. (2014). Bipolar disorder in children. *Psychiatry Journal,* 928685.

Therapeutic Research Center (2015, July; modified 2016, February). Comparison of atypical antipsychotics. *Pharmacist's Letter/Prescriber's Letter,* PL Detail-Document #310701. Retrieved September 30, 2016, from http://pharmacistsletter.therapeutic research.com

Viktorin, A., Lichtenstein, P., Thase, M. E., Larsson, H., Lundholm, C., Magnusson, P. K. E., & Landen, M. (2014). The risk of switch to mania in patients with bipolar disorder during treatment with an antidepressant alone and in combination with a mood stabilizer. *American Journal of Psychiatry, 171*(10), 1067–1073.

Acknowledgments

• • • • • • • • • • • •

I'VE BEEN ABUNDANTLY BLESSED WITH people who share a passion for healing those afflicted with bipolar disorder. Please honor with me these tremendous individuals who have helped make this book possible.

Jane Pipich, my intelligent and perceptive wife, who spent many hours with me reviewing this book, and who along with my sons Adam and Kevin, fuels me with daily love and support.

Denise Silvestro and the entire Kensington Publishing team, who have warmly welcomed me into the Kensington family, and have embraced this project with every attention to detail, so that *Owning Bipolar* can touch as many lives as possible.

Steve Harris of CSG Literary Partners, my enthusiastic agent, whose professionalism, tenacity, and positive energy leads to amazing results.

Howard Baumgarten, LPC, a master psychotherapist and owner of Smart Practice Central, who assisted in the bipolar disorder program development with great insights into mental health practice logistics, marketing, and speaking engagements.

Janet Appel, of Janet Appel Public Relations LLC, who has been incredibly gracious in providing encouragement, idea development, and media connections.

Laura Stack, the Productivity Pro, a prolific, bestselling business author and keynote speaker who provided her professional guidance in authorship with regular infusions of pure optimism.

Barbara McNichol, of Barbara McNichol Editorial, who worked diligently with me on the original manuscript, was always available to collaborate, and is completely committed to her authors' achievements.

Julie Corbett, MBA, of Authentically U Marketing, who has been relentless in promoting our mutual vision of mental health in Colorado, and who has offered valuable feedback on this project.

Katherine Claytor, MA, who encourages from a profound faith and whose input on the original draft of this book helped balance the technical information with a personal sensitivity to the reader.

Joseph Shrand, MD, a brilliant and deeply compassionate psychiatrist and author who, in addition to his distinguished professional appointments, is the award-winning author of *Outsmarting Anger: Seven Steps for Defusing Our Most Dangerous Emotion,* and *Do You Really Get Me?* as well as the founder of *Drug Story Theater: Where the Treatment of One Becomes the Prevention of Many.* He has graced us with the foreword for this book, and is simply an inspiration.

My devoted parents and all the teachers, professors, and mentors whose wisdom is never forgotten through the years.

And finally, I am forever grateful for all those who have generously shared their bipolar stories with me. Thank you to all who have submitted to BipolarNetwork.com and the Bipolar Network Facebook page, several of whom are quoted in this book. Other content originating from my thirty-plus years of mental health practice is the result of composites from various real and altered patient scenarios, along with identity changes. No matter the source or circumstance, I am deeply moved by those who have shared a part of themselves so that others may benefit.

Index

• • • •

Acceptance, x–xi, 4–6, 39–40
    of bipolar as lifelong mental illness,
        76–77
    of diagnosis and child and parent,
        181–83
    of medications, 86–89
    of new self-identity, 81–83
Adolescent patients, xiii–xv
    ADHD and, 31–32
    antisocial personality disorders and,
        34
    cyclothymia and, 17
    denial and fear of mental health
        treatment, 44–47, 50–51
    manic catalysts, 14
    medications and, 115–17
    parents, stepparents, and
        guardians, 180–86
Adult children, 186–87, 196
Aftercare plan, 163–65. *See also* Post-
    stabilization phase
Aggression, and spouses or intimate
    partners, 177–78
Alcohol (alcoholism), 36–37, 111–12, 115,
    128
Alcoholics Anonymous (AA), 164
Alprazolam, 105–6
Amygdala, 10–12, 57, 60–61
Anger, 40, 59, 76, 86, 170, 176–79
Antianxiety/anxiolytics, 105–6, 215–17
Anticonvulsants, 100–101, 102
    marijuana and, 112–13
    reference guide, 205–9
Antidepressants, 104–5, 212–14
    postpartum onset, 150
    reference guide, 212–14
    side effects, 104, 214
Antidepressives, 97, 105, 209–10

Antihistamines, 216–17
Antimanics, 97, 99, 100, 103, 105
    Cindy's story, 61–62
    reference guide, 209
Antipsychotics, 103, 209–13
Antiseizure medications, 100–103,
    205–9
    marijuana and, 112–13
Antisocial personality disorders, 33, 34
Anxiety, 14, 31, 32–33, 45, 71, 105–6
Anxiety drugs. *See* Antianxiety/anxi-
    olytics
Appetite, changes in, 26, 29
Aristotle, 199
Assessment, and first phase of care, 38,
    69–70
Athletes with bipolar disorder, 127
Attending physicians, 160–61
Attention deficit hyperactivity disor-
    der (ADHD), 31–32
Atypical antidepressants, 104–5, 212–13
Atypical antipsychotics, 103, 209–10

Baseline bipolar mood zone, 28, 30, 135
    manic experience, 55–56, 57, 60
Benzodiazepines, 215–16
Beta-blockers, 216–17
Bipolar depression
    diagnosis, 25–26
    managing negative life events, 141–44
Bipolar disorder, use of term, 9
Bipolar experience, 53–65
    Cindy's story, 61–62
    the depressive experience, 62–65
    Gloria's story, 63–64
    the manic experience, 54–62
    Maria's story, 58–61
    Ron's story, 64–65

Bipolar I Disorder, 15–16
    average age of onset, 16, 181
    diagnosing depression, 26
    diagnosing mania, 19–25
    hypercreativity and, 135
Bipolar II Disorder, 16
    diagnosing depression, 26
    diagnosing mania, 19–25
    hypercreativity and, 135
Bipolar mood zones, 27–29
    Evelyn's story, 30, 93–94
Blood tests, 78, 102
    fear of needles, 102
Brain, 10–12
    manic experience and, 57, 60–61
    medications and, 85–86
Breastfeeding, 109–10, 154–55
Buspirone, 106, 216–17

Caffeine, 128–29
Cannabidiol (CBD), 112–13
Carbamazepine, 100–101, 102, 205–6
Caregivers, support of, 187–92, 196
Case managers, 161, 164
Catalytic causes of bipolar disorder,
    13–15
Causes of bipolar disorder, 12–15
"Characterological disorders," 33
Children
    adult, 186–87, 196
    denial and fear of mental health
        treatment, 44–47, 50–51
    manic catalysts, 14
    medications and, 115–17
    parents, stepparents, and
        guardians, 180–86
Cigarette smoking, 128–29
Circadian rhythm, 130–31
Clinical trials, 86
Clonazepam, 105–6
Cocaine, 36, 113–14
Coffee, 128–29
Collaborative model of treatment, 92–
    93, 96, 161–62
College students, 186–87
Community support, 194–95
Compliance model of treatment, 91–92
Compulsive gamblers, 137
Concentration, loss off, 71, 72
Confidentiality, 49, 161, 168–69, 181
Conservatorship, 191–92
Constipation, as side effect of as med-
    ication, 107

Couples therapy, 173–75
Creativity (creative process), 3, 41–43,
    132–36
Crisis, and first phase of care, 69
Cultural biases against mental illness
    and treatment, 88
Cyclothymia, 16–17, 29

Dehydration, 97–98
Denial, 39–52, 96
    breaking through, 47–51
    as common defense mechanism, xi,
        3, 40–41, 92
    creativity and, 41–43
    mania and perceived needs, 43–44
    of mental health treatment, 44–47
    of parents, 44–45, 50–51, 180, 182, 183,
        185
    in postpartum onset, 150, 153
    in pre-stabilization phase, 71, 72
    of spouses or intimate partners, 50,
        176, 177
    in stabilization phase, 76
    Sylvia's story, 143
    Ted's story, 90
    Tom's story, 47
    your own, 51–52
Depressive experience, 62–65
    Gloria's story, 63–64
    Ron's story, 64–65
    subjective experience of being de-
        pressed, 62–63
Diagnosis, 2–3, 19–38
    of bipolar depression, 25–26
    bipolar mood zones, 27–29
    difficulty of, 3–4, 30–37
    Evelyn's story, 30
    of mania, 19–25
    Patricia's story, 37–38
Diarrhea, as side effect of medications,
    107
Diet, 126–29
Differential diagnosis, 30
Distractibility, 24, 31, 32, 70
Divalproex, 100–101, 102, 106, 205
Dizziness, as side effect of medica-
    tions, 107
Dopamine, 12, 104, 113, 128
Dreams (dreaming), 56, 57, 62
Drug abuse. See Substance abuse
Drug industry, 87
Drugs. See Medications
Dry mouth, 97–98

Dysphoric mania, 20, 23, 28, 105
Dysthymia, 28–29

Elderly patients, 117–18
Electroconvulsive therapy (ECT), 118–20
Epileptic seizures, 87, 100
"Euphoric mania," 20–21
Exercise, 126–28

Family genetics, 10, 13, 145
Family history, 13, 26, 151
Family members, 6. *See also* Family
    support
  acceptance of bipolar as lifelong
      mental illness, 76, 77
  biases against mental illness and
      treatment, 88
  caregivers, support of, 187–92
  denial of bipolar disorder, 46–47
  difficulty of diagnosis, 3–4
  expecting consistent treatment col-
      laboration, 79–80
  fears and denial of, 46–47, 50–51, 71
  medication routine, 78, 110
  postpartum bipolar and, 153
  three-phase approach to therapy,
      68, 70, 71, 73, 74, 78
  understanding the bipolar experi-
      ence, 53, 54, 55
Family support, xiv, 68, 73, 167–98
  attitude of collaboration, 161–62
  Audrey's story, 171–72
  caregivers, 187–92
  identifying and limiting supporters,
      169–70, 189–90
  knowing when to let go, 195–97
  Luke's story, 170–71
  parents, stepparents, and
      guardians, 180–87
  right to confidentiality, 168–69
  spouses or intimate partners, 173–80
  working with hospital staff, 160–61
Fear(s), xi, 5, 6
  of family members, 46–47, 50–51, 71
  of medications, 86–89
  of mental health treatment, 44–47, 49
  OCD and, 32–33
  of parents, 51, 182–83, 184
  of spouses or intimate partners, 176
"Feeling right," and medications, 107,
    109
Fight-or-flight response, 45–46
First-line treatments, 106

First phase of care. *See* Pre-
    stabilization phase
Flight of ideas, 22–23
Fountain of Youth, 126–27

Gabapentin, 208–9
Gambling compulsions, 24, 137
Genetics (genes), 1–2, 10, 13, 145
"Genius," 9, 42–43
Geriatric patients, 117–18
Goal attainment, 136–41
  Sylvia's story, 138–40
Goal-directed activities, increase in, 23
Grand Bargain, 193–94
Grandiosity, 20–21, 24, 34
Group therapy, 162–63
Guardians, support of, 180–87
Guardianship, 191–92
Guilt, 26, 71

Hand wringing, 24
Helping others, 200–201
Hemingway, Ernest, 42
Herbal remedies, 120–21
Heroin, 113–14
Homeostasis, 57, 101, 130, 141, 142, 146
Hormonal shifts, 2, 14
Hospital case managers, 161, 164
Hospital/inpatient treatment, 157–65
  attitude of collaboration, 161–62
  diagnosis, 25–26
  group therapy, 162–63
  treatment goals, 163–65
  working with hospital staff, 160–61
Hydration, 98
Hypercreativity, 3, 42–43, 135
Hypnotics, 215–16
Hypomania, 16, 28, 135

Impulsivity, 24, 60, 70, 172
Inpatient mental health treatment,
    157–60
  attitude of collaboration, 161–62
  diagnosing bipolar depression, 25–26
  group therapy, 162–63
  treatment goals, 163–65
Insomnia, 21, 26, 131
Intake counselors, 160
Intensive outpatient program (IOP), 164
Intestinal distress, as side effect of
    medications, 107
Intimate partners. *See* Spousal support
Involuntary admissions, 159

Irritability, 13, 24, 25, 34, 70, 71

Lamotrigine, 100–101, 206–7
Law enforcement, 159
Life event management, 141–44
Life values, and goal attainment, 139–40
Lithium, 95, 100–103, 204–5
    blood tests and, 78
    dosage, 205
    history of use, 67, 95
    how it works, 100–101
    as initial treatment choice, 95
    problems with, 101–2
    side effects, 108, 204
Living arrangements, 164–65
Lorazepam, 105–6, 215–16

"Madness," 9, 42–43
Mania. See also Manic experience
    ADHD and, 32
    breaking through denial, 47–49
    creativity and, 41–43
    diagnosis of, 19–25
    difficulty of diagnosis, 30–31
    Evelyn's story, 30, 93–94
    mood zones and, 28
    OCD and, 32–33
    perceived needs and, 43–44
    personality disorders and, 33
    schizophrenia and, 35, 36
    Ted's story, 89–91
    treating the symptoms, 71–72
Manic catalysts, 13–15
Manic experience, 54–62
    Cindy's story, 61–62
    Maria's story, 58–61
    Ron's story, 64–65
    subjective experience of mania, 54–55
MAOI (monoamine oxidase in-
    hibitors), 104–5, 213–14
Marijuana, 112–13
Medical algorithms, 106–7
Medical history, 13, 25–26, 37, 54, 151
Medications, x, 85–118. See also specific
    medications
    for ADHD, 31–32
    algorithms, 106–7
    children and adolescent patients,
        115–17
    Cindy's story, 61–62
    common types of, 99–106
    creative process and, 135–36
    denial and fear of, 50

dosage and side effects, 98
elderly (geriatric) patients, 117–18
Evelyn's story, 93–94
from fear to acceptance, 86–89
for long-term maintenance, 78–79
main effects of, 97
Maria's story, 58–59
"meds-only" concept, 67–68, 95–96
models of treatment, 91–93
postpartum onset, 150, 154–55
in post-stabilization phase, 78–79, 99
pregnancy and breastfeeding, 109–10
reference guide, 203–17
side effects of, 75–76, 97–99, 107–9
in stabilization phase, 73–76, 159
Steven's story, 115
substance abuse and, 110–15
Ted's story, 89–91
"Melancholia," 9
Methamphetamines, 36, 113–14
Minimization, 41, 55
Misdiagnosis, xv, 3–4, 30–37
Models of treatment, 91–93
Monotherapy, 106
Mood regulation, and neurotransmit-
    ters, 12
Mood stabilizers, 100–103, 204–9. See
    also Lithium
Mood swings, xi, 2, 10, 12, 17, 45

"Natural" remedies, 120–21
Negative life events, 141–44
    Sylvia's story, 142–44
Neuroprotective effects, 116, 136, 185
Neurotransmitters, 12, 104
Next level, 199–201
    helping others, 200–201
    personal action, 200
Nicotine, 128–29
Norepinephrine, 104, 212

Obesity, 108
Obsessive-ccompulsive disorder
    (OCD), 32–33
One Flew Over the Cuckoo's Nest
    (movie), 119
Opioids, 114
Origins of bipolar disorder, 9–12
"Out of it" feeling, 101
Outpatient treatment, 45, 163–64
"Owning" bipolar, x–xi, 4–6, 92
Oxcarbazepine, 207–8

Pain relievers, 87, 114
Parental support, 180–87
Partial hospitalization program (PCP), 164
Personality disorders, 33–34
Pleasurable activities, excessive involvement in, 24–25
Postpartum major depression, 146–47
    identifying, 147–49
    treatment, 149–55
Postpartum onset, 145–55
    breastfeeding and, 110
    identifying, 147–49
    manic catalysts for, 14
    psychiatric problems and, 37
    questions to ask doctor, 152
    treatment, 149–55
    use of terms, 145–46
Post-stabilization phase, x–xi, 77–83, 125–44
    acceptance of new self-identity, 81–83
    for all family members, 192–94
    attaining your goals, 136–41
    expecting consistent treatment collaboration, 79–80
    finding your rhythm, 126–32
    managing negative life events, 141–44
    medications in, 78–79, 99
    parents, stepparents, and guardians, 186
    spouses or intimate partners, 175–79
    treating the whole person, 80–81
    treatment goals, 163–65
    understanding the creative process, 132–36
Power of attorney (POA), 191–92
Predispositional causes of bipolar disorder, 13
Prefrontal cortex (PFC), 10–12, 57, 60–61
Pregnancy. See also Postpartum onset
    medications and, 109–10, 154
Pressured speech, 22, 36, 75
Pre-stabilization crisis, 69
Pre-stabilization phase, x–xi, 68–73
    for all family members, 192
    assessment, 69–70
    denial in, 39–52, 71
    medications in, 86–87
    models of treatment, 92–93
    spouses or intimate partners and, 175, 179
    Ted's story, 89–90
    treating the symptoms, 71–73

Productivity, 21, 41–43, 70
Projection, 41, 56, 176
Psychiatry, and medications, 87
Psychological trauma, 15, 144
Psychomotor agitation, 24, 26
Psychostimulants, 31–32
Psychotherapies, 44–45, 67–68, 92–93
    caregivers, 187–92
    Cindy's story, 61–62
    goal attainment and, 136, 139, 140–41
    Maria's story, 58–59
    "meds-only" concept, 67–68, 95–96
    negative life events and, 142–43
    parents, stepparents, and guardians, 180–87
    Ron's story, 64–65
    rules of confidentiality, 49, 168–69
    sleep disturbances and, 131
    spouses or intimate partners, 173–80
    treating the whole person, 80–81
    understanding the creative process, 132–33
Psychotic depression, 29, 35, 103, 158
Psychotic mania, 27–28, 35, 87, 135, 158

Racing thoughts, 22–23, 70
Recreational drug use, 110–14
Reference guide, 203–17
Repetitive transcranial magnetic stimulation (rTMS), 120
Restlessness, 24, 26, 71
Reward stimulation, 137–38
Rhythm in life, 126–32
    diet and exercise, 126–29
    sleep, 129–31
Risky behaviors, 24–25, 60
Roosevelt, Franklin D., 5

St. John's Wort, 121
"Sandwich generation," 188
Scapegoats (scapegoating), 88
Schizophrenia, 35–36
Second-line treatments, 106
Seizure disorders, 37
Self-doubt, 135, 142–43
Self-esteem, inflated, 20–21, 34
Self-identity, acceptance of new, 81–83
Serotonin, 12, 104
Seven bipolar mood zones, 27–29
Sexual dysfunction, as side effect of medications, 107, 108–9
Shame, 25, 56, 86, 87, 88, 90
Shrand, Joseph, ix–xii

Sibling support, 187–92
Simple denial, 41, 55
Skin rashes, 98
Sleep, 129–31
    antianxiety/anxiolytics for, 105
Sleep disturbances, 21–22, 71, 129–30
Smoking, 128–29
SNRIs (serotonin and norepinephrine
    reuptake inhibitors), 104–5, 212
Social support, 194–95
"Spacey" feeling, 101
"Splitting," 33–34
Spousal support, 168, 173–80
    interpersonal style, 176–78
    key to success, 175–76
    knowing when to let go, 196–97
    post-stabilization phase, 179–80
    pre-stabilization phase, 175, 179
    sense of validation for, 174–75
    typical issues facing, 173–74
SSRIs (selective serotonin reuptake
    inhibitors), 104–5, 212
"Stabilization," use of term, 68
Stabilization phase, x–xi, 73–77
    acceptance of bipolar as lifelong
        mental illness, 76
    for all family members, 192
    creative process and, 135–36
    diet and exercise, 127
    finding right medications, 74–76, 99
    in hospital setting, 158–59
    models of treatment, 92–93
    parents, stepparents, and
        guardians, 184–85
    spouses or intimate partners, 175–79
    treating entire disorder, 76–77
Stem cells, 10
Stepparents, 180–87
"Stigma," use of term, 87
Stigma of mental illness, xi, 87–88, 90,
    181
Stimulants, 128–29
Substance abuse, 2, 14, 17, 25, 36–37, 45,
    110–15
Sugar, 128–29
Suicide (suicidal thoughts), 4, 25, 26,
    72, 101
Super Mom identity, 148–49
Support, 167–98. See also Family support
    social and community, 194–95
Symptoms
    of bipolar depression, 26
    of bipolar mania, 20–25

bipolar mood zones, 27–29
misdiagnosis, 30–37
of postpartum onset, 147–49
treating in pre-stabilization phase,
    70, 71–73, 76

Talkativeness, 22
Tetrahydrocannabinol (THC), 112
"Therapeutic window," 101–2
Three-phase approach to therapy, x–
    xi, 67–83
    post-stabilization phase, x–xi, 77–83
    pre-stabilization phase, x–xi, 68–83
    stabilization phase, x–xi, 73–77
Thriving in life after stabilization. See
    Post-stabilization phase
Thyroid imbalances, 14, 17, 37
Topiramate, 207
Traumatic brain injury, 37
Traumatic experiences, 15, 144
    Maria's story, 58–60
Treatment
    child and parent, 183–85
    denial and fear of, 44–47
    ECT, 118–20
    goals of, 163–65
    herbal remedies, 120–21
    inpatient mental health, 157–60
    medications. See Medications
    "meds-only" concept, 67–68, 95–96
    models of, 91–93
    postpartum major depression, 149–55
    postpartum onset, 149–55
    psychotherapies. See Psychotherapies
    rTMS, 120
    three-phase approach to therapy.
        See Three-phase approach to
        therapy
Tremors, as side effect of medications,
    107
Tricyclics, 104–5, 213
Types of bipolar disorder, 15–17

Violence, 36, 177–78

Weight gain, as side effect of medica-
    tions, 107–8
Weight loss, 26
Whole person, treatment of, 80–81
Williams, Robin, 52n
Worthlessness, 26, 71

Zeta-Jones, Catherine, 41, 90–91